GOSPEL TRUTH

A Tale of the Unexpected

by

Andrew Simpson

Published by Andrew Simpson

Published by Andrew Simpson
PO Box 2856
Swindon
SN9 5WZ
England

ISBN: 0-9548367-0-7

Printed and bound by Antony Rowe Ltd, Eastbourne

By the same author:
REBECCA THE LURCHER
SUMMER PUDDING

About the author:
Andrew Simpson lives in Wiltshire.

These days he prepares texts for BBC Radio 4 (*Book of the Week, Book at Bedtime, etc*) and abridges books for the audiomarket. At an earlier stage he wrote two books which celebrate his favourite country pursuits (both still available from Tideline Books, of Rhyl, North Wales). In the very distant past he was a Classical scholar at Trinity College, Oxford. These entries in his CV allow him to hope that the brain cells remaining to him when he wrote this book were up to the job.

AUTHOR'S NOTE

The only contemporary or near-contemporary evidence relating to the Christian church in its first years is contained in the New Testament - more specifically, in the four gospels and the "Acts of the Apostles". Five short books, not many pages (120 in all, in my Bible).

I am going to base the ideas in this book exclusively on evidence existing in those five books, because, as I say, they contain the only contemporary or near-contemporary evidence available to us.

However, the New Testament is available to anyone who cares to acquire a copy. Consequently all the original evidence is available to the reader as well as to me. At every stage, therefore, he/she can look up the relevant passage and see what the text actually says. On that basis, the reader can decide whether or not I am making sense. In terms of checks and balances, this is a healthy arrangement, of which I hope the reader will take full advantage.

Dear Peter,

This slim volume should carry a Vatican Health Warning. I suggest you add it to yr library as a prized First Edition. As you are aware, reading prized first Editions is strictly verboten, because it damages the binding.

Best wishes,

Andrew

26 May 2005

CONTENTS

1. STRONG LANGUAGE

When I decided, many years ago, to learn the rudiments of the writer's trade, it came to my attention that the King James' version of the Bible (the Authorised Version) was full of excellent words and phrases, and contained an abundance of interesting imagery. It was pointed out to me that, since its completion in 1611, some of the very best writers of English have sharpened up their style by familiarising themselves with the text, and borrowing anything that they found irresistible.

"Lewd fellows of the baser sort" springs to mind. It started life in the "Acts of the Apostles", chapter 17, verse 5, and reappeared in 1899 on the lips of a schoolboy imitating a housemaster in Kipling's "Stalky & Co." – as follows:

"But to say that you stink, as certain lewd fellows of the baser sort aver, is to say nothing – less than nothing."

And this is just one example out of many. If reputable writers can resort to such tactics in the pursuit of excellence, I said to myself, so can I. The point I am trying to make is that, when a Bible took its place on my bedside table, the reason was literary and in no way spiritual.

In my youth, my spiritual influences were a mixture of the Christian and the Classical. Christian upbringing, Classical education (which is where I was introduced to the pursuit of excellence, a concept championed by Socrates). Christianity told me to behave in a particular way, because its merits were beyond doubt, after two thousand years of fine-tuning by the Christian authorities. The Classics took a different view. They suggested that one should work out the rules of behaviour for oneself.

I opted for the Classical approach, and in my twenties I cancelled the membership of a Christian church which my parents had arranged for me at the time of my birth. Since then I have found the voyage of discovery hugely satisfying. I have also been interested, and reassured, to discover that many of the fundamentals of philosophy are common ground for Muslims, Christians, Jews and Buddhists. I have yet to get to grips with Oriental philosophy, but I suspect that when I do I will find that certain principles of enlightened human behaviour are universal.

All of which is incidental, because, as I have mentioned, the Bible on my bedside table was there for aesthetic rather than moral reasons.

One night I started reading the "Acts of the Apostles", the book which comes immediately after the four gospels of the New Testament (Matthew, Mark, Luke and John). It records the Christian church's early adventures after the Crucifixion of Jesus Christ. In Christian circles it is accorded the same respect as the four gospels.

Chapter One describes how the resurrected Jesus goes up to Heaven. Then there is a meeting of the Apostles at which Matthias is elected to take the place of Judas, who, remorseful at having betrayed Jesus, has hanged himself.

Chapter Two describes the first Pentecost, when flames of fire hover over the heads of the assembled Apostles, and the Holy Spirit grants them "the gift of tongues", so people of all nationalities will understand the gospel that they are about to go out and preach. At this point my eyes began to close and I gave up the unequal struggle.

The following night I carried on. In Chapter Three, Simon Peter (now better known as Saint Peter) performs his first miracle. In Chapter Four, he is imprisoned by the Pharisees (the Jews' ruling class) for proclaiming that Jesus had risen from the dead after his Crucifixion. In court he conducts his own defence and is freed because the authorities are alarmed at the strength of the popular support he has inspired.

At verse 34 of Chapter Four, I found myself reading the following description of some of the arrangements under which the members of the early church lived:

'Neither was there any among them that lacked: for as many as were possessors of land or houses sold them, and brought the prices of the things that were sold, and laid them down at the apostles' feet: and distribution was made unto every man as he had need.... But a certain man named Ananias, with Sapphira his wife, sold a possession and kept back part of the price, his wife also being privy to it, and brought a certain part, and laid it at the apostles' feet.

'But Peter said, "Ananias, why hath Satan filled thy heart to lie to the Holy Ghost, and to keep back part of the price of the land? ... Why hast thou conceived this thing in thine heart? Thou hast not lied to men, but to God." And Ananias, hearing these words, fell down and gave up the ghost.

'And great fear fell on all them that heard these things. And the young men arose, wound him up and carried him out and buried him.

'And it was about the space of three hours after when his wife, not knowing what was done, came in. And Peter answered unto her, "Tell me whether ye sold the land for so much?" And she said, "Yea, for so much."

'Then Peter said unto her, "How is it that ye have agreed together to tempt the spirit of the Lord? Behold, the feet of them which have buried thy husband are at the door, and shall carry thee out."

'Then fell she down straightway at his feet, and yielded up the ghost: and the young men came in and found her dead, and, carrying her forth, buried her by her husband. And great fear came upon all the church, and upon as many as heard these things.'

Here we have a glimpse of the early Christian church, soon after the Crucifixion, when Jesus was no longer in charge. From this story we gather that sizeable contributions were levied from those believers who were affluent, and the money collected was distributed for the good of the church as a whole. According to the text, it was claimed by the apostle Peter (the new leader of the Christians) that this financial arrangement had Divine approval. It is clear that the threat of Divine punishment (capital punishment, in this case), and the fear which this produced, were both used to encourage compliance throughout the Christian community.

This episode intrigued me, and I wasn't sure why. Let's just say that curiosity and a sense of unease prompted me to spend some time checking back in the four gospels. I found what I was after in a story that appears in Matthew's gospel (19. 16 - 23). The same story is repeated in Mark (10. 17 - 23).

Matthew's version runs as follows: 'And behold, one came and said unto him [Jesus], "Good Master, what good thing shall I do, that I may have eternal life?" And he said unto him, "Why callest thou me good? There is none good, but one, that is God; but if thou wilt enter into life, keep the commandments." He said unto him, "Which?" Jesus said, "Thou shalt do no murder, thou shalt not commit adultery, thou shalt not steal, thou shalt not bear false witness, honour thy father and thy mother, and, thou shalt love thy neighbour as thyself."

'The young man saith unto him, "All these things have I kept from my youth up. What lack I yet?" Jesus said unto him, "If thou wilt be perfect, go and sell that which thou hast, and give to the poor, and thou shalt have treasure in Heaven: and come and follow me."

'But when the young man heard that saying, he went away sorrowful: for he had great possessions. Then said Jesus unto his disciples, "Verily I say unto you, that a rich man shall hardly enter into the kingdom of heaven. And again I say unto you, it is easier for a camel to go through the eye of a needle than for a rich man to enter into the kingdom of God." '

Here we glimpse Jesus' attitude towards materialism. He advises the young man to get rid of all his wealth. When his suggestion is not accepted, he doesn't threaten; he doesn't even remonstrate. He allows the young man to leave without so much as a word of reproach, and then uses the incident to create an anti-materialistic moral for the benefit of his disciples.

I found another passage, earlier in Matthew's gospel (6. 19 - 20), where Jesus says, "Lay not up for yourselves treasures upon earth, where moth and rust doth corrupt, and where thieves break through and steal; but lay up for yourselves treasures in Heaven."

So what had intrigued me about the "Ananias and Sapphira" story was a change of policy. During his life Jesus establishes the principle that material things should be of minimal importance to the true believer, but that it is up to the individual to make up his own mind on the subject. Within a short time of his death, however, it seems that the new management replaces this principle with something quite different.

Different, and disquieting. The account in the "Acts of the Apostles" describes a situation where the church is soliciting funds with almost indecent enthusiasm - even going so far as to insist that money shall be paid, whether the contributor likes it or not. It describes Divine punishment if payment is not made in full - there is no suggestion that the two deaths were simply an unfortunate coincidence. It also describes the use of fear of the consequences to intimidate those in the Christian community who might be unhappy about the financial arrangements which the new management has imposed.

Even if one ignores the more dramatic elements of the story - if one calls them poetic licence - one still has a problem with the basic facts. Jesus advised against materialism, Peter instituted a policy of acquisitiveness. He also claimed God's approval for a most aggressive application of this policy, whereas it is obvious that the Christian God would surely have identified with Christ's more tolerant attitude.

What was going on, I asked myself. Why am I reading a story in the New Testament which has the first Pope organizing the church's finances like Al Capone running a protection racket?

Is that analogy too strong? In both instances we have financial demands far beyond what was proper – in Capone's case it was against the law, in Peter's it was contrary to the principles Jesus had established. In both instances the demand is backed by the threat of violence, and in both instances tales of violent retribution are used to frighten the rest of the community into compliance. If Chapter Four of the "Acts of the Apostles" means what it says, Peter was indeed behaving like a gangster.

Was it possible, I asked myself, that something so apparently un-Christian could have happened at that time, in that place, among those particular people?

For the time being, I put Creative Writing on the back burner. Moral enlightenment was what I decided to seek, and I went looking for it in the pages of the four gospels, the only source of evidence about "that time", "that place", "those people".

2. CHARACTERS

The suggestion I made in Chapter One is that something fundamentally un-Christian is described in Chapter Four of "The Acts of the Apostles". The question I then found myself asking was, "Is it possible that, immediately after Jesus' death, his disciples would start changing the way his church was run in a fashion that he would have found repugnant?" This led logically to another question: "What were they like - the people who surrounded Jesus?"

Immediately I ran into Judas Iscariot. All four gospels describe how he betrayed Jesus in return for thirty pieces of silver. As a result Jesus was arrested, tried and crucified. As the story is reported in the gospels, this is an example of a man who clearly has no time for the non-materialistic principles which his master promotes. On the contrary, his number one priority is to get rich quick, and he has no scruples about how dirty his hands get in the process - until his greed results in catastrophe. Then he is overcome by remorse and hangs himself.

Let me remind you of the evidence. Consider the account given by Matthew (26. 14-16). 'Then one of the twelve, Judas Iscariot, went unto the chief priests, and said unto them, "What will ye give me, and I will deliver him unto you?" And they covenanted with him for thirty pieces of silver. And from that time he sought opportunity to betray him.'

Later in the same chapter we have the scene in the Garden of Gethsemane (verses 47 - 50).

'And while he yet spake, lo, Judas, one of the twelve, came, and with him a great multitude with swords and staves, from the chief priests and elders of the people. Now he that betrayed him gave them a sign, saying, "Whomsoever I shall kiss, that same is he: hold him fast." And forthwith he came to Jesus and said, "Hail, Master," and kissed him. And Jesus said unto him, "Friend, wherefore art thou come?" Then came they and laid hands on Jesus, and took him.'

There are two other references to Judas, both in John's Gospel.

In Chapter 12, verse 4 *et seq.*, we read, 'Then said one of his disciples, Judas Iscariot...."Why was not this ointment sold for three hundred pence, and given to the poor?" This he said, not that he cared for the poor, but because he was a thief, and had the Bag, and bare what was put therein.'

Chapter 13, verse 29, tells us, 'For some of them thought, because Judas had the Bag, that Jesus had said unto him, "Buy those things that we have need of against the feast"; or [had told him] that he should give something to the poor.'

It is clear that "the Bag" was the communal purse which provided for of the living expenses of Jesus and his disciples. It is also clear that Judas had got himself the job of treasurer, and carried out his duties in such a fashion that he was suspected by his colleagues of "fiddling". So the evidence against him is indisputable.

What were they like - the people who were close to Jesus during his lifetime? Well, there can be little doubt that Judas Iscariot was a thoroughly nasty piece of work.

*

A case can also be made against James and John, the sons of Zebedee, also known as "The Sons of Thunder".

Mark (10. 35 - 37) runs as follows: 'And James and John, the sons of Zebedee, came unto him, saying, "Master, we would that thou shouldst do for us whatsoever we shall desire." And he said unto them, "What would ye that I should do for you?" They said unto him, "Grant unto us that we may sit, one on thy right hand and the other on thy left hand, in thy glory." '

Jesus does not grant their request, and verse 41 records that, 'when the ten [the other apostles] heard it, they began to be much displeased with James and John.'

Matthew (20. 20 - 24) provides a slightly different version:

'Then came to him the mother of Zebedee's children with her sons, worshipping him and desiring a certain thing of him. And he said unto her, "What wilt thou?" She said unto him, "Grant that these my two sons may sit, the one on thy right hand, the other on the left, in thy kingdom." '

Jesus does not grant the favour, and verse 24 states: 'When the ten heard it, they were moved with indignation against the two brethren.'

It is not much, but the story makes it clear that the two sons of Zebedee were "pushy", to an extent that caused resentment among their fellow apostles, and that Jesus was unimpressed by their attitude.

Luke's gospel describes an incident that occurred when Jesus and his followers arrived at a village in Samaria, and the villagers did not make them welcome.

'And when his disciples James and John saw this, they said, "Lord, wilt thou that we command fire to come down from heaven and consume them, even as Elias did?" But he turned and rebuked them and said, "Ye know not what manner of spirit ye are of. For the Son of man is not come to destroy men's lives, but to save them." ' (Luke. 9. 54 - 6).

Here the brothers revealed themselves as more than just "pushy". They obviously had fairly extreme ideas about the lengths to which it is permissible to go in order to promote one's own interests.

So now we have three bad apples in a fairly small barrel.

*

The other apostle whose behaviour was questionable was Peter. The 26th chapter of Matthew describes (vv. 58-74) what happened after Jesus had been arrested and taken to the High Priest.

'But Peter followed him afar off unto the High Priest's palace, and went in, and sat with the servants, to see the end.... And a damsel came unto him saying, "Thou also wast with Jesus of Galilee." But he denied before them all, saying, "I know not what thou sayest." And when he was gone out into the porch, another maid saw him, and said unto them that were there, "This fellow was also with Jesus of Nazareth." And again he denied with an oath, "I do not know the man." And after a while came unto him they that stood by, and said to Peter, "Surely thou also art one of them, for thy speech bewrayeth [betrayeth] thee." Then began he to curse and to swear, saying, "I know not the man." '

This story is supported by the 14th chapter of Mark, the 22nd of Luke, and the 13th and 18th of John.

*

For the rest of the evidence concerning Peter's character, we rely on opinions expressed by Jesus himself.

In Matthew (16. 23) we read: 'But he [Jesus] turned and said unto Peter, "Get thee behind me, Satan: thou art an offence unto me: for thou savourest not the things that be of God, but those that be of men." '

In Mark (8. 33) we read: 'But when he [Jesus] had turned about and looked upon his disciples, he rebuked Peter, saying, "Get thee behind me, Satan, for thou savourest not the things that be of God, but the things that be of men." '

Then we have Luke (22. 31 - 3): 'And the Lord said, "Simon, Simon [Simon was Peter's other name], behold Satan hath desired to have you, that he may sift you as wheat; but I have prayed for thee, that thy faith fail not; and when thou art converted, strengthen thy brethren." '

Peter answered, *"Lord I am ready to go with thee, both unto prison and to death."* This, as we have seen, turned out to be just so much hot air, when push came to shove.

So Peter appears to have been a disloyal, boastful, untrustworthy man, with no great respect for truth. A man, moreover, with materialistic and worldly aspirations. Who says so? Jesus himself.

*

At this point it is only fair to put the other side of the case and to draw attention to the following passage in Matthew (16. 17 - 19): 'And Jesus answered and said unto him, "Blessed art thou, Simon Bar-Jona.... And I say unto thee that thou art Peter, and upon this rock I will build my church, and the gates of Hell shall not prevail against it. And I will give unto thee the keys of the kingdom of Heaven; and whatsoever thou shalt bind on earth, it shall be bound in Heaven; and whatsoever thou shalt loose on earth, shall be loosed in Heaven." '

Without a doubt this passage describes Peter in terms which imply that his character is admirable. However, the position of this passage in the gospel gives cause for concern, because, a mere four verses later, Jesus turns to Peter and issues the stinging and comprehensive rebuke which has already been quoted: *"Get thee behind me, Satan: thou art an offence unto me: for thou savourest not the things that be of God, but those that be of men."*

If the words with which Jesus appoints Peter head of the church are genuine, the rebuke that follows is hard to explain. By the same token, if the rebuke is genuine (and it is consistent with all the other evidence about Peter's character which we have considered), then one must have misgivings about the authenticity of the "Upon this rock" passage.

I will be saying more on this subject later on. For the moment let us accept that in Matthew (16. 17 - 19) Jesus speaks of Peter in complimentary terms.

So we have seen four passages which suggest that Peter was boastful, disloyal, and a liar. Also three passages in which Jesus says what he thinks of Peter: in two of them he describes him as excessively worldly, in the third he suggests that he will succumb to the wiles of the Devil if he doesn't pull himself together.

By contrast, we also have one passage in which Jesus appoints Peter head of the church in complimentary terms. Leaving aside my reservations about this passage, one can do the sums: the gospel evidence suggests, by seven passages to one, that Peter was far from being a saint.

*

What had I learnt about the people who surrounded Jesus? Certainly four of the original twelve apostles were of dubious character. Judas was greedy to a fault. The sons of Zebedee were ambitious to an extent that irked their companions, and seemed to think that violence was the appropriate response to even mild opposition.

Finally, Peter showed himself to be morally deficient in several respects, and appeared to be more enthusiastic about material advancement than about the spiritual principles which Jesus advocated.

Isn't this unbelievable, in a company of saints? Not really. Religious movements have always had a "worldly" dimension. In our own day, do we not regularly hear of spiritual leaders who set up shop on the basis of poverty, celibacy and self-denial, and in no time at all accumulate Rolls-Royces, girlfriends and country estates? Whenever one gets large numbers of people, from all levels of society, who fall under the spell of an idea, an individual or a group, the financial potential is obvious, and must surely appeal to the materialists among those who find themselves involved. Human nature is fairly constant: if it is true today, it would have been just as true two thousand years ago.

Besides, the gospels suggest two perfectly good additional reasons for the presence of so many suspect characters among the apostles.

3. FRINGE BENEFITS

The first of these came as a surprise to me. The four gospels revealed that there was more to Jesus' mission than the saving of souls in anticipation of an eternal hereafter. He also had designs of a more immediate and more material nature. Consider the following two passages:

1. 'And Jesus answered and said, "Verily I say unto you, there is no man that hath left house, or brethren, or sisters, or father, or mother, or wife, or children, or lands, for my sake and the gospel's, but he shall receive an hundredfold now in this time, houses and brethren and sisters and mothers and children and lands, with persecutions; and in the world to come eternal life." ' (Mark 10. 29 - 30).

2. 'And he said unto them, "Verily I say unto you, there is no man that hath left house, or brethren, or wife, or children, for the kingdom of God's sake, who shall not receive manifold more in this present time, and in the world to come life everlasting." ' (Luke 18. 29 - 30).

It is difficult to determine what exactly Jesus meant when he used terms like "houses" and "lands", and no doubt the matter has been the subject of continuous debate ever since the gospels were written.

But it is clear that those who wrote the gospels were under the impression that material reward was one of the benefits which they associated with the movement which Jesus had started. So we are looking at exactly the sort of "opportunity" that would have been likely to appeal to characters like Judas, Peter, James and John. Whether or not Jesus intended to convey this impression, I do not know. But certainly this is the impression which found its way into the New Testament.

*

The gospels also reveal that Jesus intended to do everything in his power to discomfort, and hopefully to displace, the Pharisees, who ran the Jewish nation's affairs (political and economic, as well as religious) on behalf of the Roman Empire. Historical and archaeological evidence suggests that the quality of life of these people was extremely comfortable and that the revenues they controlled were substantial.

As regards Jesus' attitude to them, consider the following: 'Then came his disciples and said unto him, "Knowest thou that the Pharisees were offended when they heard this saying?" But he answered and said, "Every plant which my heavenly father hath not planted shall be rooted up. Let them alone: they be blind leaders of the blind. And if the blind lead the blind, both shall fall in the ditch." ' (Matthew 15. 12 - 14).

Also: '"Therefore say I unto you, the kingdom of God shall be taken from you and given to a nation bringing forth the fruits thereof…" And when the Chief Priests and Pharisees had heard his parables, they perceived that he spake of them. And when they sought to lay hands on him, they feared the multitude, because they took him for a prophet.' (Matthew 21. 43 - 46).

If there is a plan to displace the ruling class of any community, those involved will be aware that the vacuum thus created must be filled by some new form of authority. When Jesus set out to discredit and displace the Pharisees, the possibility of political and material advancement for those who followed him, if his campaign were successful, must surely have been obvious, even if he himself did not intend it to be an inducement.

*

So Jesus represented (knowingly or unknowingly) the possibility of material and political rewards, as well as rewards of a purely spiritual nature. He also intended that at least some of his plans would come to fruition in the comparatively short term. Evidence of this is easy to find in the gospels.

For example: Mark (9.1):' "Verily I say unto you that there be some of them that stand here, which shall not taste death till they have seen the kingdom of God come with power." '

Matthew (10. 23) describes the instructions Jesus gives to the apostles as he sends them off to spread the word. Jesus says: "But when they persecute you in this city, flee ye to another; for verily I say unto you, ye shall not have gone over the cities of Israel, till the Son of Man be come."

*

Why so many dubious characters among the apostles? We have identified one perfectly adequate explanation: worldly, greedy and ambitious people, assessing Jesus' potential in their own worldly, greedy and ambitious terms, would have immediately spotted what may have looked like the possibility of short-term material and political advancement – if Jesus achieved his goals.

4. A SOFT TOUCH

The other explanation for the presence of suspect characters among Jesus' followers is the fact that he recruited in a manner that was casual to the point of rashness. It seems as if he simply presented his proposition to whoever he met, and whoever accepted it was made welcome. There is also evidence that some of his followers enlisted with almost indecent haste, which is marginally more likely to indicate the rogue than the saint.

An example is the case of Matthew, otherwise known as Levi, a tax-gatherer. There is nothing in his subsequent record to suggest that he was anything but a credit to the church, but the manner of his joining is, I think, significant.

Mark (2. 4) tells us: 'And as he [Jesus] passed by, he saw Levi, the son of Alphaeus, sitting at the receipt of custom, and said unto him, "Follow me." And he arose and followed him.'

No suggestion that Jesus had done any research into Matthew's character before he approached him, nor any indication that Matthew made arrangements for a replacement before he decamped. It is my impression that both recruiter and recruit were quite happy to take a chance on the outcome of the encounter, which is an exciting approach, but not necessarily a prudent one.

The recruitment of Peter is described as follows (Matthew 4. 18 - 20): 'And Jesus, walking by the sea of Galilee, saw two brethren, Simon called Peter, and Andrew his brother, casting a net into the sea: for they were fishers. And he said unto them, "Follow me, and I will make you fishers of men." And they straightway left their nets and followed him.'

The next verses read as follows: 'And going on from thence, he saw other two brethren, James the son of Zebedee and John his brother, in a ship with Zebedee their father, mending their nets; and he called them. And they immediately left the ship and their father, and followed him.'

Four more recruitments with no suggestion of any form of vetting. Also four instant enlistments: like Matthew, the parties concerned didn't seem the least bit bothered about obligations that they might have been expected to discharge before accepting Jesus' invitation. They just took off. I think it is no coincidence that three of the four fishermen turned out to be Peter and the two sons of Zebedee – three of the four suspect characters we have already identified.

*

Let me try to assemble the pieces of the jigsaw which I have identified up to this point. In the "Acts of the Apostles" we found Peter putting the squeeze on two members of the early church for money, contrary to the principles that had been established by Jesus.

"Can I believe what I am reading?" I asked myself, and did some research. The gospels suggested that I could indeed believe it. Casual recruitment and the possibility of material advancement resulted in the fact that among the twelve apostles there were four "suspect characters" of one sort or another.

The worst case was Judas, who doesn't complicate matters in the long run, because he commits suicide immediately after the Crucifixion. Second in terms of moral deficiency was Peter, whose commitment to Christ and his principles was clearly questionable. The other two were James and John, the sons of Zebedee, who were sufficiently motivated by self-interest to irritate their colleagues, and who behaved on one occasion in a manner which suggested that they had the mentality of thugs.

So the mystery is a mystery no longer. It is a fact, clearly established in the "Acts of the Apostles", that, after Jesus' death, Peter took charge of the Christian community (James and John, incidentally, were his closest colleagues). In view of what I had now established about Peter's character, the tale of Ananias and Sapphira became perfectly understandable. Peter was "worldly" during Jesus' lifetime. It should therefore come as no surprise to find him being even more "worldly" once Jesus was no longer around to restrain his materialist tendencies. Problem solved, end of story.

5. TEAM SPIRIT

So I stopped investigating and resumed my Bible reading for purely literary purposes. It was at about that time that I came across the Second Book of Kings, chapter 9, verse 20: "The driving is like the driving of Jehu the son of Nimshi – for he driveth furiously." As I had recently started playing golf, and was plagued by a devilish slice (I still am), those words made a deep impression - but that's another story.

One night I was reading the passage in Luke (5. 8 - 10) which describes how Peter first became acquainted with Jesus, after the latter had been instrumental in providing him with a bumper (and apparently miraculous) catch of fish - Peter being a fisherman, as has been mentioned.

The passage runs as follows: 'When Simon Peter saw it, he fell down at Jesus' knees, saying, "Depart from me, for I am a sinful man, Lord." For he was astonished, and all that were with him, at the draught of the fishes that they had taken; and so was also James, and John, the sons of Zebedee, which were partners with Simon.'

Immediately my detective's hat settled round my ears once again, and with some considerable force. I had had no difficulty in coming to terms with the fact that the apostles were a "mixed bag". It was simply the result of the various material and political possibilities that existed in the Christian adventure, plus the effect of casual recruitment on the part of Jesus, plus the influence of the law of averages.

But this was something new and different. I now discovered that three of Jesus' four "flawed" recruits were closely associated with each other (partners, in fact) before Jesus appeared on the scene. So it wasn't just chance that brought them into his company. It wasn't just a coincidence - three likeminded characters bumping into each other because they just happened to be in the same place at the same time. These three would have heard his proposition, and then they would have discussed it among themselves; and, being (as we have seen) interested in "bettering" themselves in the material sense, they must surely have weighed up the potential of the proposition. We know that Jesus thought he could make something out of them. Might they not have thought that they could make something out of him?

There could well be a case for giving them the benefit of the doubt and saying that they became disciples for one reason only - because the philosophy which Jesus preached inspired them to turn over a new leaf.

But if that were the case, how can one explain the fact that they were noticeably unsatisfactory (from a moral point of view) while Jesus was alive, and that, as soon as death removed him from the scene, Peter immediately started cranking up the material potential of the Christian movement - as Ananias and Sapphira discovered to their cost?

In view of these facts, I felt no enthusiasm for the benefit of the doubt. I felt that further investigation was called for – in case they were even lewder fellows of the baser sort than I already suspected.

Let me put it another way. Let's say that three young men are well-known in their community as "dodgy" rather than "straight" – which is a reasonable assumption, in view of what we know about Peter, James and John. If one of them was to volunteer for community service (good deeds, for no pay, on a regular basis), one might give him the benefit of the doubt.

"Good for him!" one might say. "Let's hope he makes something of himself."

But if all three were to volunteer *en masse*, I suspect the general reaction would be, "I wonder what they're up to!" That was certainly my reaction to the decision of Peter, James and John to become Christians.

I began to wonder whether there was any evidence in the Gospels of "group activity" by the three fishermen. If so, it would be interesting to see if they behaved like reformed characters linked only by the bonds of friendship and a shared enthusiasm for Jesus and his philosophy, or like a gang of "chancers" who had infiltrated the Christian movement in order to exploit it.

*

Reading through the four gospels I found that references to groups of apostles, identified by name, are very infrequent indeed (almost non-existent) - as far as nine of the twelve are concerned.

But the remaining three pop up four times as a group: the three being - believe it or not - Peter, and James and John, the sons of Zebedee.

So it seemed reasonable to conclude that they joined as a group, and they stuck together during the period of Christ's ministry to such a noticeable extent that their association found its way into the pages of the Gospels.

Clearly the next step was to take a close look at the passages that describe their "group" activities. I must say that I found the prospect most exciting. Remember, we are dealing with three young men who lived and died almost two thousand years ago. They feature as characters in a drama that was recorded in writing at a time when writing was a fragile and by no means reliable instrument.

From that sparse record we have already learned something about their individual characters. It now seemed likely that the record also contains anecdotal evidence which might reveal something more about them - the nature of their activities as a group. The amateur sleuth in me was fascinated by the possibilities that lay ahead.

6. THE AGE OF MIRACLES

The first of the relevant passages is Mark, chapter 1, verses 29 - 31: "And forthwith, when they were come out of the synagogue, they entered into the house of <u>Simon</u>[1] and Andrew, with <u>James and John</u>. But Simon's wife's mother lay sick of a fever, and anon they tell him [Jesus] of her. And he came and took her by the hand and lifted her up; and immediately the fever left her, and she ministered unto them."

Here we have an incident very early in Jesus' public life: he is in the company of Peter, James and John, and probably Andrew, Peter's brother, and it would seem that, in that company, he performs a minor miracle, by curing Peter's mother-in-law of a fever.

*

Next is the story of Jairus' Daughter, which is recorded in Mark (5. 22 - 43) and Luke (8. 41 - 56). The more detailed account is that of Mark.

---

[1] Peter's other name

34

'And behold, there cometh one of the rulers of the synagogue, Jairus by name; and when he saw him [Jesus], he fell at his feet, and besought him greatly, saying, "My little daughter lieth at the point of death; I pray thee, come and lay thy hands on her, that she may be healed; and she shall live."

'And Jesus went with him, and much people followed him and thronged him. And a certain woman, which had an issue of blood twelve years, and had suffered many things of many physicians, and had spent all that she had and was nothing bettered but rather grew worse, when she had heard of Jesus, came in the press behind, and touched his garment. For she said, "If I may touch his clothes, I shall be whole." And straightway the fountain of her blood was dried up, and she felt in her body that she was healed of that plague.

'And Jesus, immediately knowing to himself that virtue was gone out of him, turned him about in the press, and said, "Who touched my clothes?" And his disciples said unto him, "Thou seest the multitude thronging thee, and sayest thou, who touched me?" And he looked round about to see her that touched him. But the woman, fearing and trembling, knowing what was done in her, came and fell down before him, and told him all the truth. And he said unto her, "Daughter, thy faith hath made thee whole; go in peace, and be whole of thy plague."

'While he yet spake, there came from the ruler of the synagogue's house certain [people] which said, "Thy daughter is dead. Why troublest thou the Master any further?" As soon as Jesus heard the word that was spoken, he saith unto the ruler of the synagogue, "Be not afraid. Only believe."

'And he suffered no man to follow him, <u>save Peter and James and John, the brother of James.</u>

'And he cometh to the house of the ruler of the synagogue, and seeth the tumult, and them that wept and wailed greatly. And when he was come in, he saith unto them, "Why make ye this ado, and weep? The damsel is not dead, but sleepeth." And they laughed him to scorn.

'But when he had put them all out, he taketh the father and the mother of the damsel, <u>and them that were with him,</u> and entereth in where the damsel was lying. And he took the damsel by the hand and said unto her, "Talitha, cumi," which is, being interpreted, "Damsel, I say unto thee, arise." And straightway the damsel arose, and walked; for she was of the age of twelve years. And they were astonished with a great astonishment. And he charged them straitly that no man should know it; and commanded that something should be given her to eat.'

*

36

So, our first and second glimpses of Peter, James and John, acting as a group, reveal them as witnesses to Jesus' miraculous powers - two occasions, three miracles. It seems likely that the three apostles revealed the details of what happened in the case of Jairus' daughter after the Crucifixion, when they might reasonably have reckoned that Jesus' "gagging order" ("he charged them straitly that no man should know it") no longer applied.

*

I have no reservations about the story of Peter's mother-in-law, or the passage in the second incident which features the woman with the issue of blood, but I do have reservations about the story of Jairus' Daughter - because of that "gagging order".

As you will recall, a huge crowd accompanied Jesus to the house of Jairus. A large number of people knew what was going on, and an even larger number were about to hear all about it when Jairus' daughter, having been publicly declared dead by members of her household, emerged alive from her sick-room.

Jesus must surely have been aware of all this. So it beggars belief that he would suggest a publicity blackout about something that was already so clearly in the public domain. "He charged them straitly that no man should know it" can only make sense if Jesus was a complete idiot, which he wasn't.

There is one other way of explaining this apparent nonsense. If the story was untrue, if it was a complete invention which was circulated, on the authority of Peter, James and John, after Jesus' death, the "secrecy" element could be explained. To those who asked, "Why have we never heard this impressive story before?" the answer would be, "Because he told us to keep it quiet."

*

Would Peter, James and John have had any reason to invent such a tale? I suggest that we refer to the "Acts of the Apostles" and remind ourselves what was going on immediately after Jesus' death. The apostles were involved in a vigorous campaign of evangelism. They were spreading the word concerning Jesus, promoting him in every possible way, and they were energetically recruiting new members for the church.

38

The first aspect of this work is described in Acts, Chapter 2, verses 22 to 24, where we find Peter saying:

"Ye men of Israel, hear these words; Jesus of Nazareth, a man approved of God among you by miracles and wonders and signs, which God did by him in the midst of you, as ye yourselves also know; him being delivered by the determinate counsel and foreknowledge of God, ye have taken and by wicked hands have crucified and slain; whom God hath raised up, having loosed the pains of death: because it was not possible that he should be holden of it."

So much for the emphasis on Jesus' supernatural powers. As for the recruiting drive, verse 41 of the same chapter tells us, 'They that gladly received his [Peter's] word were baptised, and the same day there were added unto them about three thousand souls.'

In this context, there would certainly have been a motive, at that time, for "inventing" a few choice miracles. The party line was clearly to emphasise Jesus' supernatural powers.

It is also a fact that Peter, James and John were in a position to do this. They were now in authority over the Christian movement, with no Jesus around to restrain them. They had more influence than anyone else over the basic information that was included in the "authorized version" of Jesus' life and works which was circulating among the Christians, and which no doubt formed the basis for the gospels when they came to be written. If Peter, James and John wanted that information to feature miracles, it would feature miracles in abundance, whether they had happened or not.

*

So far, we have considered two stories, featuring just three miracles. Before jumping to conclusions, let us put the whole question of miracles in the New Testament under the microscope. The gospels tell us that, over a three-year period (from the day when he began to preach to the day of his death on the Cross), Jesus performed a succession of astounding feats (from transforming water into wine at the Marriage Feast of Cana, via the feeding of the 5,000 on five loaves and two fishes, to the raising of Lazarus from the dead).

The gospels also contain two passages which paint a somewhat different picture.

The first of these is in the Gospel of Mark (8. 11 - 12): 'And the Pharisees came forth and began to question him, seeking from him a sign from Heaven, tempting him. And he sighed deeply in his spirit and saith, "Why doth this generation seek after a sign? Verily I say unto you, there shall no sign be given unto this generation." '

In the previous chapter of Mark (chapter 7), we find Jesus making a dumb man talk and exorcising an evil spirit. In Chapter 6 he walks on water and feeds 5,000 people on 5 loaves and 2 fishes. In Chapter 5 he revives Jairus' dead daughter and transfers the evil spirits called Legion from a man into a herd of swine. In Chapter 4 he calms a violent storm on the Sea of Galilee. In Chapter 3 he cures many of the plague and unclean spirits fall down before him in numbers. In Chapter 2 he persuades a palsied man to take up his bed and walk, while in Chapter 1 he cures a leper and a fever victim, and exorcises an unclean spirit in the synagogue at Capernaum, under the very noses of his Pharisaic critics.

If all these miracles really happened, it is inconceivable that the Pharisees would have had the gall to ask for "a sign"; and it is inconceivable that Jesus would have responded by sighing deeply and saying that no sign was available.

But if these miracles didn't happen, how did they get into Mark's gospel?

Mark is also responsible for the second passage which casts the shadow of doubt over the miracles. He describes what happened when Jesus returned to Galilee after the journey during which the episode of Jairus' Daughter occurred. 'And he could there do no mighty work, save that he laid his hands upon a few sick folk, and healed them. And he marvelled because of their unbelief. And he went round the villages, teaching.' (Mark, 6. 5 - 6).

In view of these two passages, am I suggesting the possibility that some of the miracles which have found their way into the gospels are fairy tales dreamt up after Jesus' death? That possibility has occurred to me.

*

What did Peter, James and John get up to when they were working together? In the first two incidents described in the gospels which feature them as a group, we find them witnessing examples of Jesus' miraculous powers, and in the case of Jairus' Daughter there is textual evidence which entitles one to suspect that the story is a fabrication, and that the fabrication is the work of Peter, James and John.

There is further textual evidence which suggests that some of the other miracles described in the gospels may owe more to wishful thinking than to hard fact.

7. SIMPLY DIVINE

The third incident which features Peter, James and John is described in three of the gospels. Matthew (17. 1 - 9) provides the most detailed account, as follows:

'And after six days, Jesus taketh <u>Peter, James, and John</u> his brother, and bringeth them up into a high mountain apart. And was transfigured before them; and his face did shine as the sun, and his raiment was white as the light. And behold there appeared unto them Moses and Elias talking with him. Then answered Peter and said unto Jesus, "Lord, it is good for us to be here; if thou wilt, let us here make three tabernacles: one for thee, and one for Moses, and one for Elias." While he yet spake, behold, a bright cloud overshadowed them; and, behold, a voice out of the cloud which said, "This is my beloved son, in whom I am well pleased; hear ye him." And when the disciples heard it, they fell on their face and were sore afraid. And Jesus came and touched them, and said, "Arise, and be not afraid." And when they had lifted up their eyes, they saw no man, save Jesus only. And when they came down from the mountain, Jesus charged them, saying, "Tell the vision to no man, till the son of man be risen from the dead." '

Mark (9. 2 - 9) and Luke (9. 28 - 36) tell the same story. Like Matthew, they identify Peter, James and John as the only apostles present. They describe Jesus talking to manifestations of Moses and Elias (legendary leaders of Israel, long dead). They describe a voice from a cloud saying, "This is my beloved son", and exhorting those present to listen to him.

All three accounts shroud the incident in secrecy. Mark, like Matthew, tells us that Jesus specifically ordered his companions to say nothing about it till "the son of man were risen from the dead." Luke says, 'And they kept it close, and told no man in those days any of those things which they had seen.'

*

This is the story which has become known as "The Transfiguration". In it Jesus is described as remarkably altered in appearance, and involved in supernatural activity, communing with the spirits of the long-dead Moses and Elias. Perhaps the most important element of all is the voice from the cloud. The terms of the three accounts strongly suggest that this is the voice of God, confirming that Jesus is the Son of God, and that his words have Divine authority.

The only witnesses to this phenomenon are Peter, James and John. In two of the versions Jesus orders them to keep the event secret until "the son of man be risen from the dead." This suggests to me that the story was not made public by the three apostles concerned until after the Crucifixion.

*

If one were to ask any reputable Christian theologian to name the principles on which Christianity is based, first and foremost will undoubtedly be the belief that Jesus Christ is the Son of God, and an equal partner in a tripartite godhead (the Trinity).

Let us put this principle into context. The Buddha was a man. Mahomet was a man. Of the three great religions, only Christianity claims to have been founded by God himself. So this is no small matter.

If one then asked one's reputable theologian to explain the basis for this belief, he/she would perhaps refer to a mass of literature on the subject, the work of a host of respected authorities writing over the greater part of two thousand years. If one were to inquire about the Biblical authority which establishes and legitimises this fundamental belief, the Gospel texts describing the Transfiguration would undoubtedly be cited.

Mankind knows that Christ is God, according to Christian theology, principally because of the Transfiguration story in the Gospels - that is the bottom line; all the other arguments which claim that he was divine are essentially secondary to the Transfiguration texts.

*

So the "divinity" of Christ - perhaps the single most compelling element in the Christian religion - is based, we find, on a story revealed to the world by Peter, James and John, three men whom Jesus himself didn't trust further than he could spit. That is perhaps too strong a condemnation – let me simply say that he found all three to be unreliable in one way or another.

We also have good reason to believe that the three apostles revealed the Transfiguration story after the Crucifixion, at a time when they were busy emphasising Jesus' supernatural powers, in a promotional campaign designed to recruit new members for the fledgling church.

For both these reasons, I don't feel inclined to look upon the Transfiguration story as the last word in the debate about whether or not Jesus was God. In order to get as close as possible to the truth, I prefer to see what other evidence (if any) the gospels contain on the subject.

*

In Matthew (4. 5 - 7) we read: 'Then the devil taketh him up into the holy city and setteth him on a pinnacle of the temple. And sayeth unto him, "if thou be the Son of God, cast thyself down. For it is written, he shall give his angels charge concerning thee; and in their hands they shall bear thee up..." Jesus said unto him, "It is written again, Thou shalt not tempt the Lord thy God."'

The same conversation is recorded in Luke (4. 12).

Another relevant passage is Luke (3. 22): 'Jesus also being baptised, the heaven was opened, and the Holy Ghost descended in a bodily shape like a dove upon him, and a voice came from heaven which said, "Thou art my beloved son; in thee I am well pleased."'

What are we to make of these passages? Are we to take them literally as proof of Divinity? Or are they poetic licence?

*

There are also five passages in John, one in Matthew and one in Luke, where Jesus refers to God as "Father." (John 3.16, 8.54, 9.35, 14.10, 18.36, Matthew 26.39, Luke 10.21). However, all Christians do that to some extent ("Our Father, who art in Heaven..." for example), and it does not mean that all Christians are gods, or think they are gods. It is in fact intended to suggest the opposite - that they are very human and very frail; children, in fact, totally dependent on God, their spiritual father.

*

Next let us take a passage in John's gospel, which describes an argument between Jesus and a group of Jews. In the course of it we have Jesus saying: '"Your father Abraham rejoiced to see my day: and he saw it and was glad." Then said the Jews unto him, "Thou art not yet fifty years old, and hast thou seen Abraham?" Jesus said unto them, "Verily, verily, I say unto you, before Abraham was, I am." Then they took up stones to cast at him.' (John 8. 56 - 8).

Here Jesus uses a most dramatic and striking form of words. It is also ungrammatical and therefore not entirely easy to interpret.

"Before Abraham was, I am."

If he said those words, they certainly have a bearing on the subject we are examining.

*

We go on to seven passages in which Jesus reacts to suggestions that, in addition to being "the son of God", he is "the Christ", or "he that should come."

1. Matthew (16. 15 - 17): 'He saith unto them, "But whom say ye that I am?" And Simon Peter answered and said, "Thou art the Christ, the son of the living God;" and Jesus answered and said unto him, "Blessed art thou, Simon Bar-Jona; for flesh and blood hath not revealed it unto thee, but my father which is in heaven." '

2. Mark (14. 61 - 62): 'Again the High Priest asked him, and said unto him, "Art thou the Christ, the son of the Blessed? "And Jesus said, "I am." '

3. Luke (7. 20 - 22): 'When the men were come unto him, they said, "John Baptist hath sent us unto thee, saying, Art thou <u>he that should come</u>? Or look we for another?" And in that same hour he cured many of their infirmities and plagues, and of evil spirits, and unto many that were blind he gave sight. [Continues]

'Then Jesus answering said unto them, "Go your way and tell John what things ye have seen and heard; how that the blind see, the lame walk, lepers are cleansed, the deaf hear, the dead are raised, to the poor the gospel is preached. And blessed is he, whoever shall not be offended in me."'

4. Mark (8. 29 - 30): 'And he saith unto them, "But whom say ye that I am?" And Peter answered and saith unto him, "Thou art the Christ." And he charged them that they should tell no man of him.'

5. Luke (9. 20 - 21): 'And he saith unto them, "But whom say ye that I am?" Peter answering said, "The Christ of God." And he straitly charged them and commanded them to tell no man that thing.'

6. Luke (22. 66 - 70): 'And as soon as it was day, the elders of the people and the chief priests and the scribes came together, and led him into their council, saying, "Art thou the Christ? Tell us." And he said unto them, "If I tell you, ye will not believe: and if I also ask you, ye will not answer me, nor let me go. Hereafter shall the Son of man sit on the right hand of the power of God." Then said they all, "Art thou then the Son of God?" And he said unto them, "Ye say that I am."'

7. Matthew (26. 63 - 64): 'And the High Priest answered and said unto him, "I adjure thee by the living God, that thou tell us whether thou be the Christ, the Son of God." Jesus saith unto him, "Thou hast said: nevertheless I say unto you, hereafter shall ye see the Son of Man sitting on the right hand of power, and coming in the clouds of heaven."'

"The Christ" means "The Anointed" and is from the Greek word used in the earliest Greek versions of the Bible to translate the Hebrew original, which was "Messiah".

And what, you may well ask, was the Messiah? I claim no specialist knowledge in this area, but my research informs me that a fundamental part of the Jewish religion was the belief that a heroic figure would appear, some time or other in the future, and would bring about the ultimate salvation of the Children of Israel. That figure was the Messiah.

However, it is clear from the Old Testament that the Messiah would not be God – he would be a human being: God's instrument, certainly, but a man, for all that.

In Isaiah (45.1), Cyrus, King of the Persians, is referred to as "the Messiah", because God is going to use him as his instrument in relation to the fortunes of the Israelites. Clearly there was no question of him being anything other than human. So any suggestion that Jesus might be "the Messiah" does not necessarily imply Divinity.

The only other comment I would make about these seven passages is that in only one of the seven does Jesus unequivocally claim to be God

*

There is one other passage that relates to this subject - John (10. 33 - 38). The problem is that it is immensely obscure, and takes a great deal of reading before it starts to make sense. However, I think it justifies the effort - provided the reader only makes that effort when the brain cells are in the best possible condition. My advice would be to save it for a morning session after a good night's sleep.

The passage goes as follows:

'The Jews answered him, saying, *"For a good work we stone thee not, but for blasphemy; and because that thou, being a man, makest thyself God."* Jesus answered them, *"Is it not written in your law,* **I said, "Ye are gods'** *"? If he called them gods, unto whom the word of God came, and the scripture cannot be broken; say ye of him, whom the Father hath sanctified and sent into the world,* **'Thou blasphemest'***; because I said,* **'I am the Son of God'***? If I do not the works of my Father, believe me not. But if I do, though ye believe not me, believe the works: that ye may know, and believe, that the Father is in me, and I in him.'*

The problem is the obscurity of the text. The second sentence is too long and involved. An "if" seems to have got lost, perhaps in translation. There are semicolons where commas might perhaps have made the passage easier to understand.

In my opinion, however, the importance of this passage outweighs its obscurity, because this is the only occasion on which Jesus really gets to grips with the subject and spells out in detail what he believes is his relationship with God.

So I have attempted to turn it into clear English in order to get at the meaning. For better or for worse, the result of my efforts is as follows:

The Jews answered, "It is not for good works that we stone you, but for your blasphemy - your blasphemy being that you claim to be God, when you are just an ordinary man."

Jesus answered, "The scripture is the basis of your law and cannot be challenged. In the scripture we read, 'I said, ye are gods.' The word 'gods' is applied to people to whom the word of God came. That being so, how can you call me a blasphemer because I said I am the son of God? I have been sanctified by God and sent into the world by him. If I didn't do God's work, I wouldn't expect you to believe me. But as long as I do his work, the work should convince you of the truth; and the truth is that God is in me, and I am in him."

Jesus describes himself as someone "whom the Father hath sanctified and sent into the world." That suggests to me that he is claiming to be the servant of God, rather than his equal. He says that he is entitled to call himself "son of God" because he has dedicated himself to God's work. Without the work I am nothing, he says.

That doesn't sound like someone who thinks he is by nature Divine. It sounds like a man who has no illusions about his nature, which he accepts as being human.

The sentence, "Is it not written in your law, 'I said, ye are gods'" is a reference to the 82nd Psalm, verse 6: 'I have said, ye are gods, <u>and all of you are children of the most High.</u>' Note '<u>All of you</u>'. Clearly, therefore, the "godliness" which Jesus is claiming is not something that belongs exclusively to him. This strengthens my belief that he thought of himself as a man – a man closely linked to God only by the nature of his calling.

*

So was he God or was he not? In the Gospels, apart from the Transfiguration stories, there is a small amount of affirmative evidence - the Devil in Matthew (4. 5 – 7), the dove in Luke (3. 22), the reference to Abraham in John (8. 56 – 58) and the unqualified "I am" in Mark (14. 61 – 62).

There is a lot of evidence suggesting that he thought he was a son of God (perhaps in the same way as did every other Jew), quite a lot of evidence that he thought he might be the Messiah, a thoroughly human instrument of the Almighty.

There is also evidence in some of the passages of a diffidence in Jesus' reaction, an uncertainty, a reluctance to commit himself, when he is questioned on this subject.

Finally there is one quite interesting piece of evidence suggesting that he looked upon his work as the link between himself and the Almighty – a link which was available to anyone who was similarly dedicated.

*

We have examined the divinity of Christ in depth and in detail. Why? Because in the third example of Peter, James and John working as a team, we find that Christianity's belief that Jesus is God is based on a story which these three apostles promulgated, probably after the Crucifixion. They asserted that Jesus was indisputably God in every sense of the word, and described a scene which they (and they alone) had witnessed, a scene which featured a variety of factors which combined to suggest that Jesus was in fact Divine.

However the rest of the evidence on this subject in the New Testament is rather less positive.

8. THE ULTIMATE SACRIFICE

After the curing of Peter's mother-in-law's fever, the raising of Jairus' daughter and the Transfiguration, the fourth event in which Peter, James and John feature as a group is generally called "the Agony in the Garden" - the time Jesus spent in the Garden of Gethsemane before he was arrested, tried, condemned and executed. All four gospels describe what happened.

Mark (14. 32 - 7) tells us:

'And they came to a place which was named Gethsemane, and he saith to his disciples, "Sit ye here, while I shall pray." And he taketh with him Peter and James and John, and began to be sore amazed, and to be very heavy; and saith unto them, "My soul is exceeding sorrowful unto death. Tarry ye here and watch." And he went forward a little, and fell on the ground, and prayed that, if it were possible, the hour might pass from him. And he said, "Abba, father, all things are possible to thee; take away this cup from me; nevertheless, not what I will, but what thou wilt." And he cometh and findeth them sleeping, and saith unto Peter, "Simon, sleepest thou? Couldst thou not watch one hour?" '

Matthew (26. 37 - 40) relates the following: 'And he took with him <u>Peter and the two sons of Zebedee,</u> and began to be sorrowful and very heavy. Then saith he unto them, "My soul is exceeding sorrowful, even unto death; tarry ye here and watch with me." And he went a little further, and fell on his face and prayed, saying, "Oh my father, if it be possible, let this cup pass from me; nevertheless, not as I will, but as thou wilt." And he cometh unto his disciples and findeth them asleep, and saith unto Peter, "What, could ye not watch with me one hour?" '

Luke tells exactly the same story, without naming any apostles, and John's account is too brief to add anything to our knowledge of the matter.

*

Is this event significant?

Let us suppose for a moment that Jesus came to Jerusalem with no intention of sacrificing his life, and with every intention of continuing his ministry and extending his influence among the Jews, to the disadvantage of the Pharisees.

On his arrival he is acclaimed by enormous crowds (Matthew 21. 6 – 12, Luke 19. 29 – 38), and he signals his serious intent by expelling the traders and money-changers from the temple (Matthew 21. 8 – 13). Everybody is agog to see what he will do next, and his many followers are convinced that, as a result of his intervention, life is going to be significantly improved for everybody.

If, after all that, he is simply arrested, tried, condemned and executed, without there being any mitigating factor which could reduce the demoralising impact of this disaster on his followers, that would probably have been the end of Christianity – nipped in the bud, never to be heard of again.

The mitigating factor, the extra circumstance which allowed his death to be, not a disaster, but a triumph, was the belief that the Crucifixion was part of his plan, part of God's plan, which involved nothing less than the redemption of mankind from sin through Christ's voluntary sacrifice of himself on the cross. In those terms, his death could be seen as an inspiring step in the right direction, rather than as the ultimate calamity.

And that is the view that prevailed: his death was hailed as a triumph, and that belief became (and remains) one of the central pillars of Christianity – primarily on the basis of the two passages quoted at the beginning of this chapter.

It is interesting to find Peter, James and John featuring in yet another incident which had, and continues to have, such immense significance in the shaping of Christian belief. However, the evidence of their participation is vague, as you can see. Jesus took the three of them with him when he first arrived in the garden, but then he left them and "went forward a little" before his "Agony" began.

When he rejoined them, they were asleep. So it is hard to judge to what extent they were eye-witnesses of what transpired. We don't even know if they were within earshot. However, it is likely that the story of what happened was originally related by one or other of the three (or all of them in concert), because the rest of Jesus' entourage was even further away during the crucial period, and there is no evidence that Jesus himself talked about the matter.

I see little point in speculating about the role of the three apostles in this drama, for the reason I have just mentioned – it is impossible to define exactly what part they played in the event described. Instead I prefer to stand back and ask the general question: did Jesus die willingly, or did he not - what else do the gospels tell us?

*

The evidence against the proposition consists of two accounts of his last moments on the cross.

'And at the ninth hour Jesus cried with a loud voice saying, "Eloi, Eloi, lama sabachthani," which is, being interpreted, "My God, my God, why hast thou forsaken me?" ' (Mark 15. 34).

Then there is Matthew (27. 46): 'And about the ninth hour Jesus cried with a loud voice, saying, "Eli, Eli, lama sabachthani." That is to say, "My God, my God, why hast thou forsaken me?" '

These passages, unless I am vastly mistaken, describe a person who is anything but content to accept what is happening to him. To me he sounds incredulous, shocked and disappointed.

*

On the other side, we have the Gethsemane story. Three of the four accounts make it abundantly clear that Jesus approached his own demise, and the suffering that would be part of the process, as a willing participant, because it was part of a plan of which he approved.

In addition, there are at least five passages in the Gospels (two each in Matthew and Mark, one in Luke), in which Jesus reveals, well in advance, what is going to happen to him, and makes it clear that he is a willing participant in developments which include his own death.

In Matthew (16. 21) we read: 'From that time forth began Jesus to show unto his disciples, how that he must go unto Jerusalem, and suffer many things of the elders and chief priests and scribes, and be killed and be raised again the third day.'

Four chapters later (20. 18 - 19), Jesus says: "Behold we go up to Jerusalem, and the son of man shall be betrayed unto the chief priests and unto the scribes, and they shall condemn him to death, and shall deliver him to the Gentiles to mock and to scourge and to crucify him; and the third day he shall rise again."

Nothing could be more explicit. Jesus looks ahead, with equanimity, to arrest, execution, and resurrection.

Mark, chapter 9 (31 - 32), reads: 'For he taught his disciples and said unto them, "The son of man is delivered into the hands of men, and they shall kill him; and after that he is killed, he shall rise the third day." But they understood not that saying, and were afraid to ask him.'

In Mark's 10th chapter (33 - 34) Jesus says: "Behold we go up to Jerusalem; and the son of man shall be delivered unto the chief priests and unto the scribes; and they shall condemn him to death, and shall deliver him to the Gentiles; and they shall mock him, and shall scourge him and shall spit upon him and shall kill him; and the third day he shall rise again."

In both passages Jesus patently accepts the prospect of arrest, execution, and resurrection. In the first, the writer adds that his followers did not understand what Jesus was saying.

Finally we have Luke (18. 31 – 34): 'Then he took unto him the twelve and said unto them, "Behold we go up to Jerusalem, and all things that are written by the prophets concerning the Son of man shall be accomplished. For he shall be delivered unto the Gentiles, and shall be mocked and spitefully entreated, and spitted on. And they shall scourge him and put him to death; and the third day he shall rise again." And they understood none of these things: and this saying was hid from them, neither knew they the things that were spoken.'

Again we have Jesus accepting the prospect of arrest, ill-treatment, execution and resurrection.

Luke adds, and emphasises, that the significance of Jesus' words was lost on his hearers at the time. This (and the similar passage in Mark referred to above) I find puzzling. Is it possible that they failed to understand a message of such importance, conveyed in such clear terms?

*

On balance, however, most of the evidence supports the proposition that Jesus died willingly and had familiarised his disciples with the sequence of experiences he was about to undergo (arrest, trial, ill-treatment, execution, death and resurrection) well before that sequence began. He had also, according to the gospels, made it clear that he was a willing participant in what was about to happen.

So, in spite of the presence of Peter, James and John, and in spite of the fact that the "willing self-sacrifice" story is just the sort of thing that they would have been tempted to invent, I was quite content to accept the Gethsemane story as genuine, because it is so comprehensively and unambiguously supported by so many other passages in the Gospels.

'From that time forth began Jesus to show unto his disciples, how that he must go unto Jerusalem, and suffer many things of the elders and chief priests and scribes, and be killed and be raised again the third day.' What could be more explicit than those words of Matthew's Gospel?

9. CURIOUSER & CURIOUSER

A few days after I had reached this conclusion, and was preparing to sum up the evidence relating to Peter, James and John, I started to read Chapter 20 of John's gospel, which describes what happened three days after the Crucifixion:

'The first day of the week cometh Mary Magdalene early, when it was yet dark, unto the sepulchre, and seeth the stone taken away from the sepulchre. Then she runneth and cometh to Simon Peter, and to the other disciple, whom Jesus loved, and saith unto them, "They have taken away the Lord out of the sepulchre, and we know not where they have laid him."

'Peter therefore went forth and the other disciple, and came to the sepulchre. So they ran both together, and the other disciple did outrun Peter, and came first to the sepulchre. And he, stooping down and looking in, saw the linen clothes lying; yet went he not in.

'Then cometh Simon Peter following him, and went in to the sepulchre, and seeth the linen clothes lie, and the napkin that was about his head, not lying with the linen clothes but wrapped together in a place by itself. Then went in also that other disciple, which came first to the sepulchre, and he saw, and believed. For as yet they knew not the scripture, that he must rise again from the dead.'

They knew not the scripture that he must rise again from the dead. Really? Well, that is fascinating! No doubt one could argue indefinitely about the meaning of the term "the scripture", but it makes no difference to the basic meaning of the passage: the three people involved appeared to be amazed to find the tomb empty.

This creates a strange inconsistency.

We have identified five passages in which Jesus predicted his death, and described what was going to happen to him, in detail, for the benefit of his followers; each passage describes the resurrection as part of the process. And these passages are the fundamental reason for believing that Jesus died willingly.

Yet here we are told that neither Peter, nor Mary Magdalene, nor "the apostle that Jesus loved" had any foreknowledge of the Resurrection. If that was so, there cannot have been any advance notice of Jesus' acceptance of death as a fate to which he was resigned - because all five of the relevant passages contain details of every stage of the final drama of his life: arrest, mistreatment, execution on the cross, <u>and resurrection</u>. If they hadn't been notified in advance about the Resurrection, it is fair to conclude that they hadn't been forewarned about the rest of the process. So this inconsistency is not just strange – it is massive.

It suggests that all the "early warning" passages are bogus, fabricated after the event.

But if one eliminates them from the equation, the only reason for believing that Jesus sacrificed himself voluntarily is the Gethsemane story.

So once again we appear to have a fundamental feature of Christianity – one of the Crown Jewels of the faith - and once again it seems highly likely that it is based exclusively on the word of Peter, James and John.

*

I looked further, and I found more. In Mark (16. 9 - 13) we read: 'Now when Jesus was risen [from the grave] early the first day of the week, he appeared first to Mary Magdalene, out of whom he had cast seven devils. And she went and told them that had been with him, as they mourned and wept. And they, when they had heard that he was alive, and had been seen of her, believed not. After that he appeared in another form unto two of them, as they walked and went into the country. And they went and told it unto the residue: neither believed they them.'

There is more. In Luke (24. 10 - 11) Mary and several other women bring the news of the resurrection to the disciples. 'And their words seemed to them as idle tales, and they believed them not.'

The gospels are telling us that, immediately after the death of Jesus, his followers behaved as if the Crucifixion had come as a huge shock, and the Resurrection as a complete surprise. Yet they also tell us that Jesus repeatedly gave these very followers prior notice of both these events.

I find that very odd. I suspect that someone has been telling untruths and encouraging untruths, and eventually authorising untruths to be put in writing – and has been rather careless about concealing the inconsistencies that expose the untruths for what they are. It is difficult for a written lie to be convincing if it is surrounded by passages which discredit it - as is the case in this instance.

In my opinion, the reaction of the rank and file among the followers of Jesus indicates the true state of affairs. They wept at his death and they were incredulous at talk of his resurrection. This can only mean that he had said nothing to prepare them for the Crucifixion or the Resurrection.

If that is so, then the passages in which Jesus forewarns his followers of his death, and the Gethsemane story, in which he acquiesces in his demise, are fabrications, composed after the Crucifixion and probably designed to salvage a considerable triumph out of what was in fact an unmitigated disaster.

An unmitigated disaster, which Jesus recognised as such, when he cried out, "My God! My God! Why hast thou forsaken me?"

10. A PIECE OF MY MIND

Let us sum up the "group" activities of Peter, James and John.

In the matter of miracles, they promote Jesus as a miracle-worker. There is alternative evidence in the gospels which suggests that many of the miracle stories are fabrications.

In the matter of "divinity", we only have the word of Peter, James and John for the core evidence which suggests that Jesus was God. There is alternative evidence which indicates that he wasn't, and that he himself did not subscribe to the belief that he was "divine."

In the matter of "voluntary death", it seems highly likely that Peter, James and John were the only apostles in a position to provide the core evidence supporting the belief that Jesus died of his own free will, namely the Gethsemane story.

My original inclination was to find nothing suspicious in the participation of "the three" in that incident, because there was plenty of alternative evidence supporting the "voluntary death" theory.

We now discover evidence strongly suggesting that all that supporting evidence is unreliable, most probably concocted after Jesus' death. On balance, therefore, the Gospels suggest that Jesus probably did not die willingly, and that Peter, James and John invented the idea that he did.

*

I have presented all the Gospel evidence concerning Peter, James and John with as much objectivity as I can muster. It is now up to the reader to draw his/her own conclusions.

I myself am persuaded by the evidence which suggests that Jesus was a man, not a God. Apart from the Gospel evidence, I have two reasons for this. First, Jesus said things which clearly indicate that he expected "the Kingdom of God" to be established in his lifetime (as detailed in Chapter Three). Two thousand years on, we know that he was wrong about this. Gods do not make such mistakes.

Second, if Jesus was God, and his three-year ministry was God's major effort to redeem the human race, it has to be said that it was strangely ineffective. We are perhaps further from Salvation now than we were in the pre-Christian period. Clearly, therefore, the career of Jesus did not amount to a major intervention on the part of the one true God.

Moving on, I side with the Gospel evidence that he was not a miracle worker, although it is highly likely that he was a faith healer, whatever that may be. I am happy to admit that this is not a subject of which I have expert knowledge

I also believe that when Jesus made his final visit to Jerusalem he had no intention whatsoever of dying on the Cross. Again, I am relying on evidence in the gospels - evidence which is available for all to see. On the one hand, evidence that he did not wish to die. On the other, evidence that the passages which support a "willing victim" theory are fabrications.

*

In my view, Jesus captivated his original followers because of his philosophy and because of his personality, without resorting to magic, without making claims of divinity, and without assuming the role of the sacrificial lamb. These were all - in my opinion - myths invented after his death.

Since his death, his philosophy has continued to attract vast numbers of people, of all races, in spite of negative factors – not of his making - which I shall bring to the readers' attention in due course. And during the two thousand years since his time on earth no one has improved on his attempt to make sense of the human condition, though many have tried.

His influence for good has taken its place effortlessly among the greatest that mankind has ever experienced. He is on a par with Buddha and Mahomet, with Socrates, Aristotle and Confucius. I only recently discovered that Jesus Christ is respected by Buddhists and has a place of honour in the literature of Islam. That adds an extra dimension (not that he needs one) to the reverence he inspires. Such a man, in my opinion, does not need a pack of lies to sustain him.

*

It is also my opinion that Peter and the Sons of Zebedee were "on the make" from the moment they became followers of Jesus, and that, as soon as he died, they stepped in, while everyone else was in a state of shock, and established themselves as the governing body of the church. It wasn't just Peter, thrown in at the deep end and doing his best in difficult circumstances; it was a triumvirate of like-minded men, long accustomed to working together, and determined to have their way.

Their objective was to salvage the fragile organisation which had fallen into their hands, and which was of importance to them in one or possibly two ways: first, it contained a philosophy which they may well have found attractive; second, it certainly represented the best career prospects they had ever had.

Their strategy was to promote the attractions of the Christian movement, and they started with a series of immensely impressive exaggerations and falsehoods. I have no doubt that they "invented" Jesus' divinity, his miraculous powers and his "voluntary" death.

In the short term, these falsehoods must certainly have boosted the morale of the first Christians. In the longer term, however, the Christian religion has been severely handicapped by the fact that some of its fundamental beliefs (based on these falsehoods) are clearly suspect, and, in the view of many, patently unsustainable.

There is also the very important matter which first drew my attention to Peter's behaviour: the story of Ananias and Sapphira. This is a fully-documented case not of snatching a fantasy out of the air but of changing the rules which Jesus had clearly advocated.

Peter didn't agree with Jesus' principles concerning materialism, so he ignored them and instituted arrangements which suited him better. This set a precedent which was to be of immense significance; a precedent which I will bring to the readers' attention in due course.

*

It may come as a surprise to the reader to find that I have a certain amount of sympathy and respect for Peter and his two closest colleagues.

They were liars, cheats, untrustworthy, and "on the make". But after the Crucifixion they didn't run away from what was a dangerous situation – any one of them could have been the next victim of Pharisaic revenge or Roman justice.

The fate of Peter is shrouded in obscurity. One tradition has it that he died a martyr's death in Rome, another that he died in his bed of natural causes at a ripe old age.

Most traditions have it that John retired to the island of Patmos and lived out his life in peace and quiet. His brother James, on the other hand, was executed by Herod Agrippa in 42 AD because of his Christian activities, which is a stark reminder of the risks all three faced.

So if one is going to censure them for the liberties they took, one must also acknowledge their resourcefulness, one must give these three "lewd fellows of the baser sort" credit for their resilience in dangerous times. And I do.

Virtually the first thing Peter says to Jesus in Luke's gospel is, "Depart from me, for I am a sinful man, O Lord." (5. 8). If we take that as an honest admission, we have no right to expect angelic behaviour from him and his friends when they are left holding the baby, so to speak. However, that makes no difference to the fact that they were the last people who should have been allowed to get their hands on a magnificent philosophy at a time when it was at its most vulnerable.

11. SECRETS OF THE GRAVE

There is no gospel evidence which ties Peter, James and John to the Resurrection. However, it can't be ignored. After all, if I am right in suggesting that Jesus didn't have a divine nature or miraculous powers, the Resurrection simply couldn't have happened. I have also suggested that Peter, James and John did all that they could to ensure that the Crucifixion should be looked on as a triumph rather than a disaster. In that context the Resurrection is a major factor. So what was the truth of the matter? Do the gospels give any clues?

The tale is told in some detail in Matthew's 27th chapter (verses 57 - 61). From this we learn that Jesus was crucified on "the preparation day" (the day before the Jewish Sabbath), and died some time during that evening. Joseph of Arimathea, one of his followers, had asked Pontius Pilate, the Roman Governor, if he could see to the burial of the body, and Pilate had agreed. The body was put into a tomb belonging to Joseph that same evening (the evening of "the preparation day"), and a stone was rolled against the entrance.

Matthew (27. 62 – 66) continues as follows: 'Now the next day, that followed the day of preparation, the chief priests and Pharisees came together unto Pilate, saying, "Sir, we remember that the deceiver said, while he was yet alive, 'After three days I will rise again.' Command therefore that the sepulchre be made sure until the third day, lest his disciples come by night and steal him away, and say unto the people that he is risen from the dead; so the last error shall be worse than the first. Pilate said unto them, "Ye have a watch; go your way; make it as sure as ye can." So they went and made the sepulchre sure, sealing the stone and setting a watch.'

It is interesting to note that, according to this account, the Pharisees knew that Jesus had predicted his resurrection. This is at odds with the statement in John's gospel that Peter, Mary Magdalen and "the apostle that Jesus loved" knew of no such prediction when they were faced by the empty tomb. It is also at odds with the passages which describe the incredulity of the majority of the other apostles when the resurrection was announced.

We have seen other passages where the Resurrection is allegedly predicted in advance, and the overwhelming evidence suggests that these were fabrications concocted after the event. It is quite likely that this instance is more of the same. I know what I think, and I leave it to the reader to make up his or her own mind about the matter.

There can be little room for argument, however, about four other points in Matthew's narrative. First, the body was handed over to one of Jesus' supporters and was placed in a tomb belonging to him. Second, the body lay unguarded for one night. Third, there is no evidence that anyone checked to see if the body was still in the tomb when the stone was eventually sealed and the watch was set. Fourth, it is clear that the Pharisees considered it likely that an attempt would be made to steal the body.

By the next morning the body of Jesus was no longer in the tomb, and nobody had seen it go.

Mark (ch. 16), Luke (ch. 24) and John (ch. 20) tell of a rolled-back stone, an empty sepulchre and angels announcing the resurrection.

Matthew (28. 2 - 4) describes an earthquake during the night, and the stone rolled back by an Angel of the Lord, whose presence caused the guards to 'shake and become as dead men.'

Seven verses later he says (11 - 15): 'Some of the watch came into the city, and showed unto the chief priests all the things that were done. And when they were assembled with the elders and had taken counsel, they gave large money unto the soldiers, saying, "Say ye, His disciples came by night, and stole him away while we slept..." So they took the money and did as they were taught; and this saying is commonly reported among the Jews until this day.'

*

The gospels, therefore, tell us that a divine Jesus rose miraculously from the dead. The gospels also tell us that the dead body of a human Jesus (if that is in fact what he was) was so situated after the Crucifixion that stealing it away would have been comparatively easy – for the leaders of the Christian community. They also tell us that rumours abounded that that is exactly what happened.

All in all, therefore, the gospel accounts of the Resurrection are acceptable to those who believe Jesus was God, and to those who don't. They provide ammunition for both sides.

Granted the views I have previously expressed, it will come as no surprise to the reader to discover that I reject the "miraculous" explanation, and have no doubt that in fact Peter and his colleagues were responsible for "the Resurrection" during the first twenty-four hours after the body's entombment.

*

I think Peter, James and John – all credit, once again, to their boldness – stole the body of Jesus and announced "the Resurrection". It was a masterstroke. It presented the members of the shattered Christian community with a story which they wanted to believe more than anything in the world. So they swallowed it, hook, line and sinker.

The myth-making that followed became child's play once the Resurrection had been achieved. The first myth: Jesus worked miracles, and had actually restored Jairus' daughter to life.

"That's news to us," is the general reaction.

"We saw it with our own eyes," confirm Peter, James and John.

"Why did you not tell us at the time?"

"He told us not to."

The second myth: Jesus had foretold his death, which was consequently not a tragedy at all, but part of his plan. This "spin" resulted in the passages in the gospels in which Jesus warned his followers that he was to be executed and that he would rise from the dead - passages which make no sense whatsoever when assessed alongside the passages which tell us that his death brought his followers to the brink of despair, and his "resurrection" came as a complete surprise to them.[2]

The third myth: Jesus was God, and had revealed his divine nature to Peter, James and John at the Transfiguration. When this claim is first made, once again the natural reaction is, "Why have we never heard of this before?" "Because he asked us to keep it secret until after the Resurrection" comes the reply.

As "the Resurrection" had apparently just occurred, the Divinity of Christ was accepted without question and the story of the Transfiguration immediately took its place in authorized Christian literature.

As a consequence of all this, institutional Christianity has been squarely based on a pack of lies from the moment of Jesus' death up to the present day, which is a pity.

---

[2] Such a muddle might even have inspired someone to create the legend that, although Jesus repeatedly foretold his fate in the clearest terms, his Apostles simply failed to understand him!

12. WHO WROTE THE SCRIPT?

Now for something different. Lenin, the founding father of the Communist movement, didn't approve of Stalin. On his death-bed he wrote what has been described as his "political will and testament". In it he recommended that Stalin should not take over from him, because he was, in Lenin's view, "too brutal." Lenin died, and Stalin used his immense powers of persuasion to get himself the top job in spite of Lenin's warning.

Lenin was right – Stalin was too brutal, and he was responsible for by far the worst disaster the human race has ever endured. More people suffered worse misery for longer at his hands than at the hands of any other human monster before or since. And it happened because a comparatively virtuous man died prematurely, and his authority fell into the hands of a villain – does that ring a bell?

That's not the end of the story. Stalin understood the nature of "the masses". He was aware that they needed a Father-figure (or even a God-figure); an object of worship and a source of reassurance. So he created an aura round the figure of the late lamented Lenin, for that purpose.

Lenin's writings, however, were subjected to the most ruthless censorship. Stalin only allowed the public to read those elements which fitted in with his own plans, while the residue (which didn't) were air-brushed out of existence - which brings us back to Jesus and his legacy.

As Stalin deified Lenin, so Peter deified Jesus. The question arises: did he also censor and/or re-write Jesus' teachings to suit the policies which he was in the process of imposing on the Christian community?

I decided to find out – if it was possible. It seemed like the logical next step in the process I had initiated.

My plan was to assemble the passages in the four Gospels which would seem to convey the essence of the philosophy Jesus advocated. Once assembled, they could be put under the microscope, to see if there was any evidence that someone other than Jesus had had a hand in their composition.

How would I tell? Well, as a basic first step, I would simply apply to the assembled passages the knowledge concerning Jesus, on the one hand, and Peter, James and John, on the other, which I had acquired during the investigation so far.

If I found Jesus advocating fire and the sword as the way to respond to those who did not immediately accept his teaching, the thought would certainly cross my mind that such sentiments were rather more typical of James and John than of Jesus. If I found him advocating materialism as a priority, Peter would undoubtedly spring to mind.

And if I found Jesus suggesting that his word was law because he was God (and capable of violent retribution if provoked), it would remind me that the three apostles were very positive about Jesus' divinity (and about the Almighty's appetite for retribution), whereas Jesus himself was rather ambivalent on the subject of his own essential nature, and a model of tolerance towards those who didn't see things exactly as he did.

That was the process which I planned to apply to the passages which are assembled in the next few pages.

MATTHEW

(Ch. 5, v. 1 – 10) Blessed are the poor in spirit, for theirs is the kingdom of heaven. Blessed are they that mourn, for they shall be comforted. Blessed are the meek, for they shall inherit the earth. Blessed are they that hunger and thirst after righteousness, for they shall be filled. Blessed are the merciful, for they shall obtain mercy. Blessed are the pure in heart, for they shall see God. Blessed are they that are persecuted for righteousness' sake, for theirs is the kingdom of heaven.

(5. 39) Resist not evil: but whosoever shall smite thee on thy right cheek, turn to him the other also.

(5. 44) Love your enemies, bless them that curse you, do good to them that hate you, and pray for them which despitefully use you, and persecute you.

(6. 14) If you forgive men their trespasses, your heavenly Father will also forgive you.

(6. 19 – 21) Lay not up for yourselves treasures upon earth, where moth and rust doth corrupt, and where thieves break through and steal: but lay up for yourselves treasures in heaven, where neither moth nor rust doth corrupt, and where thieves do not break through nor steal: for where your treasure is, there will your heart be also.

(6. 25) Take no thought for your life, what ye shall eat, or what ye shall drink; nor yet for your body, what ye shall put on. Is not the life more than meat, and the body than raiment?

(7.1) Judge not, that ye be not judged.

(7. 5) First cast out the beam out of thine own eye, and then shalt thou see clearly to cast out the mote out of thy brother's eye.

(12. 31) All manner of sin and blasphemy shall be forgiven unto men: but the blasphemy against the Holy Ghost shall not be forgiven unto men.

(15. 1 – 2) Then came to Jesus scribes and Pharisees, saying: 'Why do thy disciples transgress the tradition of the elders? For they wash not their hands when they eat bread....' (v16) And Jesus said... (vv19, 20) 'Out of the heart proceed evil thoughts, murders, adulteries, fornications, thefts, false witness, blasphemies. These are the things which defile a man: but to eat with unwashen hands defileth not a man.'

(16. 26) For what is a man profited if he shall gain the whole world, and lose his own soul?

(18. 4) Whoever shall humble himself as this little child, the same is greatest in the kingdom of heaven. And whoso shall receive one such little child in my name, receiveth me.

(18. 21 – 22) Then came Peter to him and said, 'Lord, how often shall my brother sin against me, and I forgive him? Till seven times?' Jesus saith unto him, 'I say not unto thee, until seven times: but, until seventy times seven.'

(19. 18 – 19) Thou shalt do no murder, thou shalt not commit adultery, thou shalt not steal, thou shalt not bear false witness, honour thy father and thy mother; and, thou shalt love thy neighbour as thyself.

(19. 21) If thou wilt be perfect, go and sell that thou hast, and give to the poor, and thou shalt have treasure in heaven: and come and follow me.

(22. 37 – 39) Thou shalt love the lord thy God with all thy heart, and with all thy soul, and with all thy mind. This is the first and great commandment. And the second is like unto it, Thou shalt love thy neighbour as thyself.

(23. 11 – 12) But he that is greatest among you shall be your servant. And whosoever shall exalt himself shall be abased; and he that shall humble himself shall be exalted.

(23. 13) But woe unto you, scribes and Pharisees, hypocrites! For ye shut up the kingdom of Heaven against men: for ye neither go in yourselves, neither suffer ye them that are entering to go in.

(25. 34 – 40) Then shall the King say unto them on his right hand, 'Come ye blessed of my Father, inherit the kingdom prepared for you from the foundation of the world. For I was an hungred [one who hungered], and ye gave me meat: I was thirsty, and ye gave me drink: I was a stranger, and ye took me in: naked, and ye clothed me: I was sick, and ye visited me: I was in prison, and ye came unto me.' Then shall the righteous answer him, saying, 'Lord, when saw we thee an hungred, and fed thee? Or thirsty, and gave thee drink? When saw we thee a stranger, and took thee in? Or naked, and clothed thee? Or when saw we thee sick, or in prison, and came unto thee?' And the King shall answer and say unto them, 'Verily I say unto you, Inasmuch as ye have done it unto one of the least of these my brethren, ye have done it unto me.'

MARK

(Ch. 3. 28 – 29) Verily I say unto you, all sins shall be forgiven unto the sons of men, and blasphemies wherewithsoever they shall blaspheme; but he that shall blaspheme against the Holy Ghost hath never forgiveness, but is in danger of eternal damnation.

(7. 6) Well hath Isaias prophesied of you hypocrites, as it is written, 'This people honoureth me with their lips, but their heart is far from me.'

(7. 21 – 23) From within, out of the heart of men, proceed evil thoughts, adulteries, fornications, murders, thefts, covetousness, wickedness, deceit, lasciviousness, an evil eye, blasphemy, pride, foolishness; all these evil things come from within, and defile a man.

(8. 36) For what shall it profit a man, if he shall gain the whole world, and lose his own soul?

(9. 35) If any man desire to be first, the same shall be last of all and servant of all.

(9. 43) And if thy hand offend thee, cut it off: it is better for thee to enter into life maimed, than having two hands to go into hell.

(10. 18 – 21) And Jesus said unto him... 'Thou knowest the commandments, Do not commit adultery, Do not kill, Do not steal, Do not bear false witness, Defraud not, Honour thy father and thy mother.' And he answered and said, 'Master, all these have I observed from my youth.' Then Jesus, beholding him, loved him, and said unto him, 'One thing thou lackest: go thy way, sell whatsoever thou hast, and give to the poor, and thou shalt have treasure in heaven.'

(11. 25) And when ye stand praying, forgive, if ye have ought against any; that your Father also which is in heaven may forgive you your trespasses.

(12. 30 – 31) And thou shalt love the lord thy God with all thy heart, and with all thy soul, and with all thy mind, and with all thy strength: this is the first commandment. And the second is like, namely this, Thou shalt love thy neighbour as thyself. There is none other commandment greater than these.

LUKE

(6. 27 – 28) Love your enemies, do good to them which hate you, bless them that curse you, and pray for them which despitefully use you.

(6. 36 – 37) Be ye therefore merciful, as your Father also is merciful. Judge not, and ye shall not be judged: condemn not, and ye shall not be condemned: forgive, and ye shall be forgiven.

(6. 42) How canst thou say to thy brother, 'Brother, let me pull out the mote that is in thine eye,' when thou thyself beholdest not the beam that is in thine own eye? Thou hypocrite, cast out first the beam out of thine own eye, and then shalt thou see clearly to pull out the mote that is in thy brother's eye.

(7. 47) Her sins, which are many, are forgiven, for she loved much.

(9. 25) For what is a man advantaged, if he gain the whole world, and lose himself, or be cast away?

(9. 62) No man, having put his hand to the plough, and looking back, is fit for the kingdom of God.

(10. 25-28) And, behold, a certain lawyer stood up, and tempted him, saying, 'Master, what shall I do to inherit eternal life?' And he said unto him, 'What is written in the law?' And he answering said, ' Thou shalt love the Lord thy God with all thy heart, and with all thy soul, and with all thy strength, and with all thy mind; and thy neighbour as thyself.' And he said unto him, 'Thou hast answered right: this do, and thou shalt live.'

(12. 1) Beware ye of the leaven of the Pharisees, which is hypocrisy.

(12. 10) And whosoever shall speak a word against the Son of man, it shall be forgiven him: but unto him that blasphemest against the Holy Ghost, it shall not be forgiven.

(12. 15) Take heed, and beware of covetousness, for a man's life consisteth not in the abundance of the things which he possesseth.

(12. 22 – 23) Take no thought for your life, what ye shall eat; neither for the body, what ye shall put on. The life is more than meat, and the body is more than raiment.

(14. 11) For whosoever exalteth himself shall be abased; and he that humbleth himself shall be exalted.

(14. 33) Whosoever he be of you that forsaketh not all that he hath, he cannot be my disciple.

(17. 3 – 4) If thy brother trespass against thee, rebuke him; and if he repent, forgive him. And if he trespass against thee seven times in a day, and seven times in a day turneth to thee, saying, I repent, thou shalt forgive him.

(18. 20) And a certain ruler asked him, saying, 'Good Master, what shall I do to inherit eternal life?'

And Jesus said unto him, 'Thou knowest the commandments, Do not commit adultery, Do not kill, Do not steal, Do not bear false witness, Honour thy father and thy mother.' And he said, 'All these have I kept from my youth up.' Now when Jesus heard these things, he said unto him, 'Yet lackest thou one thing: sell all that thou hast and distribute unto the poor, and thou shalt have treasure in heaven.'

JOHN

(4. 23 – 24) The true worshippers shall worship the Father in spirit and in truth: for the Father seeketh such to worship him. God is a Spirit: and they that worship him must worship him in spirit and in truth.

(6. 27) Labour not for the meat which perisheth, but for that meat which endureth unto everlasting life, which the Son of Man shall give unto you.

(8. 4 – 11) They say unto him: ' Master, this woman was taken in adultery, in the very act. Now Moses in the law commanded us, that such should be stoned; but what sayest thou?' .... But Jesus... said unto them, 'He that is without sin among you, let him first cast a stone at her.' ... And they which heard it, being convicted by their own conscience, went out one by one.... and Jesus was left alone, and the woman.... He said unto her, 'Woman, where are thine accusers? Hath no man condemned thee?' She said: 'No man, Lord.' And Jesus said unto her, 'Neither do I condemn thee. Go, and sin no more.'

(8. 32) And ye shall know the truth, and the truth shall make you free.

(10. 11) I am the good shepherd; the good shepherd giveth his life for the sheep.

(13. 14 – 15) If I then, your Lord and Master, have washed your feet, ye also ought to wash one another's feet. For I have given you an example, that ye should do as I have done to you.

(14. 16 – 17) And I will pray the Father, and he will give you another comforter, that he may abide with you for ever; even the Spirit of truth.

(15. 13) Greater love hath no man than this, that a man lay down his life for his friends.

(15. 17) These things I command you, that ye love one another.

(18. 37) To this end was I born, and for this cause came I into the world, that I should bear witness unto the truth.

*

Based on the passages quoted, here is my analysis of the principles which the Gospels say Jesus espoused:

The importance of love (love of God, love of one's neighbour, love of one's enemy).
The importance of forgiveness - God is forgiving, man must be equally so.
The importance of a man's soul.
The importance of self-respect (whatever one's station in life).
The importance of tolerance.
The importance of commitment.
The importance of truth.

The insignificance of material things, and of the superficial.
The iniquity of spiritual pride, hypocrisy, abuse of power, murder, adultery, theft, fraud and false witness.

The infinite mercy of a benevolent God.

*

Are the words we read in the gospels the real thing? Are they all his own work? Do they convey everything which he advocated?

Harking back to the tests to which I planned to subject the evidence, do we find Jesus backing up his recommendations with threats of violent retribution against those who are not persuaded by him? By no means. No threatening, no bullying.

The only time he gets savage is in regard to "the sin against the Holy Ghost." No one is quite sure what that is. In all probability, it is the abuse of power by those in authority, when they mislead those who look to them for guidance. If that is the case, anger cannot be seen as a major feature of his teaching, as far as the ordinary Christian is concerned. On the contrary, the keynote of his message to "the common man" is one of forgiveness.

*

Do we find him advocating materialism? Far from it: he consistently describes material things as being of no value whatsoever.

*

Does he reinforce his injunctions by reference to the supernatural, the miraculous, the divine? Does he say, "I am God, so be sure and do exactly what I tell you – or else!"? Far from it. He offers ideas and propositions - ideas and propositions that have to make sense if they are to command respect. We have already heard him saying, "If I do not the work of my Father, believe not me."

*

What we find is, in my opinion, all his own work. Should there be more – have bits been removed? It is impossible to be sure, but what we have is comprehensive. Its implications cover every aspect of human behaviour.

*

Finally, is the philosophy described in the Gospels exciting enough to have inspired those who first heard it with the enthusiasm which is described in the Gospels?

In those days, in the uncompromising world of the Roman Empire, might was right, life was hard, and the lot of the common man was no bed of roses. In that context, a philosophy which was based on love and forgiveness, and which raised the poor and the meek to a place of honour in the human pecking order must have been beyond the wildest dreams of the great majority of those who heard Jesus preach. To my mind, all the elements required to create great excitement in such an era are still discernible in the pages of the Gospels.

It is my conclusion, therefore, that the philosophy of Jesus survives essentially intact and uncontaminated in the gospels. I'm not surprised. It was his philosophy which attracted people in the first place, and Peter would not have done anything to diminish that attraction. He strikes me as having been bold enough to crank up the allure of his "Messiah" by tales of the supernatural, but far too shrewd to risk tampering with the original message which had proved so immensely powerful well before the cranking-up was effected.

Besides, Peter didn't feel the need to change Jesus' teachings. If he found them inconvenient, he simply ignored them - as in the case of poor Ananias and Sapphira. His rule of thumb seems to have been that the Christian community was welcome to the words of the Master, provided that this did not in any way restrict Peter's determination to do things his way.

13. WHY SO PALE & WAN?

We have good grounds for believing that Jesus' philosophy inspired those who first heard it with an extraordinary enthusiasm. We have also established that in all probability this philosophy survives intact in the pages of the gospels.

I ask myself: does it have the same magic today that it seems to have had when first offered for public consumption? It is an interesting point. On the one hand, familiarity breeds contempt, and the Christian world has been familiar with the contents of the Gospels for two thousand years, seven days a week and often twice on Sundays. As a result, it would not be surprising to find that Christ's words and ideas have lost some of their original impact.

In addition, much has changed in two thousand years. It is not impossible that yesterday's answer to mankind's problems may look pitifully inadequate in this day and age.

Against that, modern man is more embarrassed than he has ever been by his palpable failure to learn how to behave. In recent times two world wars, the nuclear threat, political instability, famine, disease and our ever-more frantic attempts to turn Planet Earth into a toasted crisp suggest that we are getting worse rather than better.

In that context, the Christian ideal is even more attractive now than it ever was – for those who still take optimism seriously; and I suspect that today's average man would give his eye teeth for a life which incorporated the principles that Christ advocated, and for a chance to make progress towards the blessings that he promised were achievable.

If that is even halfway to being a reasonable appraisal of the situation, why aren't the Christian churches humming with excitement, bursting with energy and moving mountains in their determination to make the world a better place? Why are they empty? And why are many of the people who used to visit them disappointed, disillusioned and apathetic?

*

My answer is that those who succeeded Peter at the head of the Christian community simply stuck to his policy. They ignored Jesus' principles whenever they found them inconvenient, and promoted principles of their own devising.

So the inspiring contribution of the Master is reduced to a purely decorative role and is overshadowed, obscured, smothered for all practical purposes, beneath a philosophical framework that has become, by and large, uninspiring - because its creators have been thoroughly uninspiring people.

Let me put the matter in some sort of context, by comparing the origins of Christianity with those of Buddhism and Islam. Buddha began to preach when he was 35. He died when he was 80. He spent the 45 intervening years improving and adapting and explaining his philosophy, until it was as he wanted it to be – in theory and in practice. As his death approached, he is quoted as saying, "What I have taught and laid down as Truth and Discipline, this will be your Master when I have gone."

Mahomet began the creation of the Islamic religion in about 610 AD. He spent the next 22 years improving the basic design. During the last few years of his life he was the most powerful man in the Arab world. So he had ample opportunity to ensure (as far as these things are possible) that his philosophy was clearly defined by the time of his death.

In contrast, Jesus had just three years at the head of the movement which he founded. He was then executed, with little or no chance of establishing exactly what the Christian philosophy meant, or exactly how it should be applied in the daily life of the ordinary man and woman.

If that wasn't enough of a disadvantage, we also have good reason to believe that control over his message fell into the hands of the three apostles who were least likely to understand what he had in mind, least likely to respect his wishes, and most likely to abandon his principles if they fancied doing things differently.

*

If Peter, James and John changed the rules, which they did, it is not surprising to find that the hierarchy which succeeded the Apostles followed suit. It would have been the easy option, and its provenance must have seemed unquestionable. If Peter managed church affairs in such-and-such a way (his successors might well have reflected), who are we to do things differently?

To put the matter in practical terms, it is my contention that, if Jesus had been around when Peter was extorting money from Ananias and Sapphira, he would have stopped him in his tracks, and if he had in fact appointed Peter head of the church (which I doubt), he would have sacked him on the spot. I would also suggest that, if Jesus had survived for a few more years than he did, he would have established a pattern of Christian principles, at all levels, which would have been significantly different from the one which actually emerged.

But he didn't survive, and in his absence the church went off at a tangent, and that divergent tendency has continued ever since. Roman Catholicism must take most of the blame, simply because it <u>was</u> Christianity throughout the period when deviations were taking root. However, I doubt if there are many Christian churches in existence today which do not carry the mark of Peter's handiwork and attitude somewhere in their arrangements.

However, the scenario which I have just described is worthless unless I can identify a significant catalogue of instances where the Christian Church has authorised, promoted and implemented principles and practices that Christ himself would have found unacceptable. This I will now try to do, and the reader can decide whether or not I make my case.

14. CHANGE AND DECAY?

Jesus said, "Suffer little children, and forbid them not, to come unto me: for of such is the kingdom of Heaven." (Matthew. 19. 14). As a sentiment, it is not difficult to understand. Children = innocence + limited opportunities, as yet, for behaving badly. So they are at their most angelic and one can see them fitting into a heavenly environment with the minimum of difficulty.

Strangely enough, the church took a different view. Children, the church decided, did not belong in Heaven in their natural state, whatever Jesus might have said. If a child died before being baptised by a priest, that child was doomed to the gloom of "limbo", for all eternity. As far as I know, this is still the view of the Roman Catholic Church.

This was just one application of an immensely powerful device to which the early Christian Church resorted (and one which is still operating): Original Sin.

The theory is as follows: because Adam and Eve disobeyed God by eating the apple in the Garden of Eden, the human race became "tainted by sin" and none of Adam's descendants were eligible for any sort of happiness, earthly or heavenly, unless they qualified for the benefits of redemption which Christ made available by his death on the Cross. The only way they could qualify for redemption was – predictably – by joining the Christian Church and complying with its requirements!

For the best part of two thousand years, Christian civilisation has been bedevilled by the notion that human nature is basically unsound, and by the belief that countless generations were "tainted by sin", and seriously disadvantaged, simply because the Book of Genesis states that the first man and his wife did a naughty deed.

It is a laughable idea (both morally and scientifically), but untold millions have fallen for it, because they looked to the Church for guidance and trusted the guidance they were given.

But surely, it is reasonable to suggest, the Church must be able to call on the authority of Jesus Christ for a principle as significant as "Original Sin".

Not a bit of it. One can read the Gospels from end to end without ever finding Jesus suggesting that mankind carries this unfortunate handicap in his DNA.

In the Old Testament, Genesis tells us that Adam and Eve were thrown out of the Garden of Eden for their disobedience, and that life outside was harder than the life to which they had become accustomed, but that does not amount to mass-contamination of the whole species.

So how did Original Sin find its way into the Christian canon? I understand it was the brainchild of St Paul. The "Acts of the Apostles" tells us about him in some detail. He was a Jew of Tarsus (21.39), and also a Roman citizen (22.25). He had the education and upbringing of a Pharisee (26.5). When he first appears, he is called Saul and is involved in the persecution of the early Christians (7.58). He is then converted, in a miraculous context (9.3), and becomes a Christian, and for reasons which are not explained changes his name to Paul (13.9).

It is my understanding (although I am by no means an authority on this subject) that the experts in this field point to Paul's Epistle to the Romans, chapter 5, verses 12-21, as the significant passage in the New Testament as far as Original Sin is concerned.

It is long, and confused, and by no means clear, but the essential sentences are as follows: "Wherefore, as by one man sin entered into the world, and death by sin; and so death passed upon all men, for that all have sinned... Nevertheless death reigned from Adam to Moses, even over them that had not sinned after the similitude of Adam's transgression, who is the figure of him that was to come. But not as the offence, so also is the free gift. For if through the offence of one many be dead, much more the grace of God, and the gift by grace, which is by one man, Jesus Christ, hath abounded unto many."

In my humble opinion, that is very near to being incomprehensible. However, according to the accepted wisdom it means that Adam's transgression (eating the apple) made the whole human race sinful, and Christ's death on the cross redeemed us from that handicap, provided that each and every individual submitted to due process of redemption, so to speak, which could only be carried out by the Church.

One can see the attraction of such a theory, as far as the leaders of the Church were concerned, in the days after the Crucifixion. As has been mentioned, at that time it was important that Christ's death should appear to have been a triumph.

Therefore it would help if it had achieved something marvellous. Let us suppose that the simple fishermen are scratching their heads over this one, when along comes the highly-educated Pharisee from Tarsus.

"He redeemed the whole human race," says Paul.

"Redeemed the whole human race from what?" asks Peter.

"From the taint of sin," says Paul, "which has been the human condition since Adam and Eve ate the apple."

In a nutshell, Paul simply invented Original Sin. It provided glorious justification for the death on the Cross, and, almost incidentally, it gave the Church a psychological stranglehold over the Christian community, because absolution from "the taint" could only be achieved with the Church's blessing.

In the early days there were Christians who didn't accept this notion. They were not convinced that Adam's guilt could be passed on to descendants who could not possibly be held responsible for his wrongdoing.

On the face of it, one would be inclined to agree. How can one be guilty of something which happened before one was born? More to the point, how can a just and loving God apportion guilt in such an unjust and unloving way?

However, the Fathers of the Church persisted with the hard line, and over a period of centuries the dissenters were hounded out of the Christian fellowship. As a result, "The Fall", "the weakness of the flesh", "the old Adam", or simply "human nature" have become accepted in the Christian world as bywords for innate depravity. The whole of Western civilisation has been affected by this crushing psychological handicap, which has been enthusiastically exploited by generations of churchmen to frighten their congregations into doing what they are told.

So Jesus Christ encouraged his followers to feel good about themselves (unless and until they mess up), while his church decided that all men are doomed – unless and until the church decrees otherwise. This must surely rank as one of the greatest deviations in the history of philosophy.

[The principle that underpins it is easy to understand: the more you frighten people, the easier it is to control them. "You're doomed from the start, as are your children – unless and until you toe the line" is not exactly reassuring. On the other hand, the more you frighten people, the less Christian you become.]

*

Jesus said, "All sins shall be forgiven unto the sons of men... But he that shall blaspheme against the Holy Ghost hath never forgiveness, but is in danger of eternal damnation." The church didn't quite see it that way. No sins are forgiven unto the sons of men, said the church, unless and until they have received absolution from a priest. As for "eternal damnation" – the ultimate punishment became applicable to a wide variety of sins, at the discretion of the clergy.

*

Jesus said, "Lay not up for yourself treasures on earth." Whereupon the Catholic Church accumulated one of the largest fortunes in the history of the world, and set an example which has been followed by numerous other so-called Christian denominations.

Christ also said that one cannot "serve God and Mammon." It is clear that in his view a very rich church will have difficulty in arranging its priorities.

However those who claimed to speak in his name decided that this injunction was one which could safely be ignored – and a certain amount of confusion regarding its priorities has indeed manifested itself over the centuries. Here we have another deviation of enormous significance.

*

Jesus made it his business to attack immorality and malpractice by those in high places – witness his vitriolic criticisms of the Pharisees. The Church spent the two thousand years after his death turning a blind eye to corruption in its own ranks and in shamelessly compromising with the "worldly" powers with which it coexisted. Obviously the latter practice makes life safer and easier, but I cannot find any passages in the Gospels where Jesus suggested that following in his footsteps would be either safe or easy.

*

Jesus said, "If I do not the work of my Father, believe not me." He preached truth, logic, commonsense. The Church opted for a regime based on edict, backed by threats. Eventually the Catholic Church devised the principle of Papal Infallibility - anything the Pope says is true, and no one is allowed to argue, on pain of excommunication, with "eternal damnation" no doubt waiting further down the line for those who persist in arguing. Can divergence be any more extreme?

And if the church was ruthless in its reaction to criticism from the rank and file of the Christian community, it was twice as ruthless in crushing criticism from within its own hierarchy. This created a culture of blind and unquestioning obedience imposed on the laity by an organisation that was itself addicted to more blind and unquestioning obedience within its own ranks.

It would be hard to imagine anything more sterile, or anything more diametrically opposed to the philosophy of the founder than this perverse pattern developed by his so-called followers. In fact I believe he had something to say on the subject:

'If the blind lead the blind, both shall fall into the ditch.' (Matthew 15. 14)

*

Jesus promised bliss in the hereafter; but he also insisted that every effort be made to create heaven on earth. The Church retained his bold words on paper, but very soon stopped trying to deliver the promise which they convey. Instead it simply defined life on earth as a "vale of tears" and instructed the faithful to expect nothing to smile about, on this side of the grave.

As for the major moral judgements that have to be made at frequent intervals by all human communities, the Christian Churches tend to leave those to the secular authorities, almost as if moral judgements are none of their business. It is not hard to imagine the contempt with which Jesus would surely have viewed this mean-spirited abdication of responsibility.

*

Finally the early Christian Church made saints of Peter, James and John, even though the New Testament tells a different story, as we have seen. Human nature being what it is, this development is understandable. Those who sanctified the Big Three were their successors. If they had denounced them, they would have been undermining their own legitimacy.

Princes of the church seldom indulge in such heroics, and this refusal to face the truth continues to the present day. As a result Christianity is fundamentally flawed by the legacy which Peter, James and John left behind, and which has been given a place of honour by those who came after them: a legacy of unsustainable claims and indefensible practices.

*

The blame does not lie with the people. In spite of the system of spiritual blackmail which the hierarchy imposed, it wasn't long before the rank and file began to suspect that they were being cheated, and made their feelings known.

The Reformation was the manifestation of widespread disgust at the corruption which, by the Middle Ages, was rife in the Catholic Church. It succeeded in fragmenting Christianity, and it may have had some impact on the behaviour of priests, bishops and popes, but it made little difference to the fact that many of the principles which the church was implementing and imposing on the faithful were principles which Jesus would never have sanctioned.

*

The problem is not limited to the Roman Catholic Church. Consider the Church of England, which is disproportionately influential, having put down roots all over the world as a result of Britain's imperial expansion. Since its establishment the Church of England has been a puppet in the hands of government.

Up to a point, this is understandable. The Church of England inherited from the Catholic Church a long tradition of compromising, of running away from confrontation, and of treating its own material welfare as the number one priority.

One has a certain sympathy with it in its early days. It was founded by Henry VIII on the understanding that it would do what it was told or suffer the consequences – and Sir Thomas More was just one of many who paid with his life for defying the king. However, those days are long gone, and still the Church of England is as timid as a mouse. But there is a price to pay for playing the game by Peter's rules rather than by Jesus' – in the shape of empty churches. And the Church of England is paying that price with a vengeance.

Only recently did I learn that Leo ("War and Peace") Tolstoy was excommunicated by the Russian Orthodox Church for criticising it in print. Among other things, he wrote, "I became convinced that the Church's teaching, although it calls itself Christian, is that very darkness against which Christ strove and ordered his disciples to strive."

And again: "The Church, acknowledging Christ's teaching in words, directly rejected it in life." (Both from "What I Believe", 1884.)

If the same charges can reasonably be levelled (and have been levelled) against Roman Catholicism, English Protestantism and the Russian Orthodox Church, I think it fair to claim that fundamental and damaging changes have been made to the basic principles of the religion which Jesus gave to the world, and that much of so-called Christianity is Christian only in name.

It is not surprising, therefore, that congregations have dwindled. As the "product" became progressively more and more repressive and less and less inspiring, deviating further and further from the original concept, Christians became less and less enthusiastic. Who can blame them?

15. LOGICAL CONCLUSION?

When I set out to discover why Peter was so unpleasant to Ananias and Sapphira in the "Acts of the Apostles", I had no idea where the trail was going to lead. Now that I have reached the end of it, I look back and am delighted at what I have discovered. I am sure that Ananias and Sapphira are equally delighted. They have been waiting two thousand years for someone to blow the whistle on Peter. The whistle is now well and truly blown. Peter (and his two partners) can be seen in their true colours. While paying lip-service to the principles which Jesus advocated, they moved the goalposts as and when they felt like it – and those who followed them followed suit. As a result, the Christianity that developed was a rather gaudy, but at the same time rather anaemic, imitation of the original.

However the state of play that has developed is interesting, to put it mildly. Because, although true Christianity was for all practical purposes shelved by the deviant tendency, it appears that it is still intact and readily available in the pages of the Bible, gathering dust.

So my conclusion is not simply a case of pointing the accusing finger at those reprehensible executors who so wantonly wasted the priceless legacy of the crucified Jesus. This is the exception to the rule – a misappropriated legacy which was not squandered, but was simply buried.

As I see it, there is no insurmountable obstacle to digging up, dusting off and putting back into service. There could well be a case for so doing. The gap in the market is plain to see: throughout the world hundreds of millions of disappointed Christians are itching for a philosophy which meets their needs, which the existing manifestations of their faith clearly do not.

A re-launch of the original model would be relatively easy. As a first step, all that is required is that the obvious falsehoods be eliminated from the formula, along with the beliefs and practices which are based on them.

That first step should prove a delight and a relief. I can think of nothing more re-invigorating for the Christian community than release from the crushing burden of impossible expectations. This will be achieved as soon as Miraculous Powers, Divinity, Resurrection and the concept of the Sacrificial Lamb are removed from the blueprint.

After that, all that is required is the abolition of those rules, regulations, concepts and attitudes (particularly attitudes) which are the legacy not of Jesus but of generations of Christian *apparatchiks* whose priority has always been to look after their own interests, rather than to promote the welfare of the Christian community.

Once those two steps have been taken, the fossilised Christianity which has alienated so many becomes a thing of the past, and one can look to the Gospels for the original ideas and instructions which a great philosopher recommended to mankind as a basis for true happiness – ideas and instructions which uplifted and inspired the vast majority of those who first received them, and which continue to attract, in spite of the restrictions placed on them by those who claim to hold "the keys of the Kingdom."

In the short term, there is every good reason for moving in that direction. Never has Christianity – in fact never has mankind - been so obviously in need of all the help it can get in managing its affairs. We haven't been so clever in the last two thousand years that we can afford to turn our back on a recipe that might just be a lifeline for a struggling species on an endangered planet.

Nor should one overlook the fact that, in addition to improving the human condition in the here and now, the ideas and instructions of Jesus Christ provide a valid passport to bliss in the eternal hereafter - if it turns out that there is such a thing. That's belt and braces insurance of the very highest class - what more could anyone ask?

Looking at the matter from another point of view, I can think of nothing more depressing than the prospect of another two thousand years during which mankind continues to be deprived of real Christianity simply because the modern equivalent of the Pharisees find their own deviant versions easier to manipulate, and because the Christian rank and file let them get away with it.